Visions of Jesus

Charlotte Patricia Lambert

Copyright

© 2018 Charlotte Patricia Lambert. All rights reserved.

ISBN: 978-0-620-80634-3

Visions of Jesus

Jesus is beautiful. He is majestic, yet loving. Sovereign in power, yet kind and gentle. He is seated in heavenly places, yet he can sit beside you when you eat. He soars in the air, up in the heavens, yet he walks beside you.

All rights reserved. No part of this publication may be reproduced or transmitted in any form or by any means, electric or mechanical, including photography, recording or any information, storage and retrieval system, without permission in writing from the publisher.

CONTENTS

Chapter One   Page 11
The river of God's Spirit

Chapter Two   Page 15
The Source

Chapter Three   Page 19
Deliverance

Chapter Four   Page 29
Servitude

Chapter Five   Page 33
The river in the book of Ezekiel

Chapter Six   Page 40
His Word

Chapter Seven   Page 46
**I The fountain II Spiritual Interpretation
III Reasons IV Advice**

Chapter Eight   Page 50
**I The Father's hand II The fire and the blood III Grace IV Glory
V Encouragement**

Chapter Nine   Page 55
I Obedience II The presence of God

Chapter Ten   Page 59

I The Old church II Dry land and

the promise III Shepherds of the flock

Chapter Eleven   Page 64
I Jesus' love II Call to ministry

Chapter Twelve   Page 67
Psalm 1

Chapter Thirteen   Page 70
I Waiting on God II The Lord in Glory

Chapter Fourteen   Page 74
I Life; goals and achievers

II The beautiful cloth

Chapter Fifteen   Page 81
I The Great white throne

II Feeding the sheep III Youth ministry

Chapter Sixteen   Page 86
Earthly blessings from heaven

Chapter Seventeen   Page 88
I A vision of heaven II The glory

and us on earth

Chapter Eighteen   Page 91
I The glory of God in us II Altar call

III The purpose of the glory

Chapter Nineteen   Page 94

Freedom; humility and reward

Chapter Twenty   Page 98
I What we eat   II New names

Chapter Twenty One   Page 102
I Alone   II Storms in a fountain

III Coldness

Chapter Twenty Two   Page 108
I Being touched   II Christmas gifts

III Pearls of love

Chapter Twenty Three   Page 111
I His majesty and us   II Promise of

redemption   III Holy of Holies

Chapter Twenty Four   Page 115
Cleansing and Perseverance

Chapter Twenty Five   Page 121
Fully blessed

Chapter Twenty Six   Page 126
I The impact of war   II Gifts   III Victory

over a demon

Chapter Twenty Seven   Page 131
I Protection of an angel   II The anointing

and the anointed   III Unity

Chapter Twenty Eight   Page 136

I Who's will? II The gift of marriage

Chapter Twenty Nine   Page 140
I Be encouraged II Relationships in

Christ III Moving into the mission field

Chapter Thirty   Page 146
I Baptism II End time signs

III Filled and rained upon

Chapter Thirty One   Page 158
I A happy family II Your calling

III Definition of the number Twelve

Chapter Thirty Two   Page 165
I The way up II Royal gown colors

and fabric III Frozen growth

Chapter Thirty Three   Page 168
I Strange planets II Signs in the sky

Chapter Thirty Four   Page 171
I A personal touch from God II Healing

through an angel III Spiritual growth

IV Words of encouragement

Author biography   Page 177

One Month Journal   Page 182

ACKNOWLEDGMENTS

First of all I want to thank God Almighty for the supernatural inspiration and guidance I needed to write this book. It is not a work of my own talents or imagination. I merely recorded what I saw and heard. Even the scriptural references came through divine guidance. I only followed the instructions.

I wish to thank Pastor Alain Bagaya of Acts Christian Church in Midrand, for presenting me with a computer to complete this book. I also wish to thank everyone at Acts Christian Church, for your love and support over the years. May God richly bless you.
Authoress.

A new move of the Holy Spirit.

Events during the period 1996-2012.

Every couple of years something new happens in the spiritual realm, when God shows us that He does new things all the time. So we should never think that we can place Him inside a box and limit His activities. We should allow Him to renew us continually; each time we find ourselves stuck in our ways.

This is the recounting of a series of divine events, which occurred during one such period of a special outpouring of the Holy Spirit.

Special Terminology:
In some places in the book the words "brother" or "sister" are used. These words refer to born-again members of the family of God.

Scriptural references in this book are mainly taken from the NIV Bible. A few are from the Good News Bible.

Cover design: Author

Foreword

In our Christian walk we need to meet Jesus and we need to find out more about him. We need to walk with him, talk to him, listen when he speaks, confide in him, trust him and seek his beautiful face.

Jesus has the most beautiful eyes I have ever seen. His eyes are full of love and deep compassion. In my visions, which usually occur during my times of worship, I see Jesus in gowns of amazing colours. Mostly the gowns have golden borders around the hem and the sleeves.

The gowns come in colours like: cerise pink, soft hues of blue, soft yellow, cream white and pure white.

Sometimes the gowns are floral. The floral prints on these gowns are of brilliant and breathtakingly beautiful colours. Sometimes Jesus holds a huge diamond in his hands. This diamond is magnificently brilliant, with the colours which it reflects. It is bigger than the size of an egg. The diamond seems to contain various powers. I am convinced in my spirit that it contains the power of everything we may ever need in life: healing, healthy self-esteem, love, talent, joy, peace, hope, perseverance, creativity and every other good gift.

In some visions Jesus is riding high up in the sky, above everything else, because he is above all earthly circumstances. He already has the victory and it is eternal.

In some visions Jesus sits on a throne and he is wearing a crown filled with many precious stones of various colours. The entire area around the throne shines, engulfed in a bright white light.

Authoress

I sincerely think that the book will be a benefit to many, I have therefore given my full approval of it:
Alain Bagaya, zone Pastor and Bible school Dean: Acts Church, Midrand.

Part 1
Dedication

For Gerald, Henry, Charl and Marvin. I love you, always. Be true to yourselves.

CHAPTER ONE

The river of God's Spirit

On the morning of 27 September 1998, during Sunday morning worship at my local Church in Pretoria, South Africa, I had the following vision:
1. a. I saw copper pots at the bottom of a river, where the currant is still. The pots are full and the other water flows over them and is meters above their tops, reaching the banks of the river. I also saw other pots bobbing about, near the surface of the river and they are only partially filled.

In a spiritual sense this showed me the full extent to which we have to be submitted to the flow of the Holy Spirit. Before the pots sink to the bottom they are filled completely.

This is a point where believers are fully submitted to the working of the Holy Spirit in their lives and few of us reach this point. Yet, to me this special place in a believer's life symbolizes the equivalence of our complete blessing in Christ, as portrayed in Psalm 23 verse 5, (the latter part): "You anoint my head with oil, my cup overflows". This would indicate a situation of being filled with the Holy Spirit, in the same way as a pot is being filled with water from the river. With the filling of the Holy Spirit comes the anointing upon our lives.

Anointing is traditionally done with oil. The oil anoints the head. When the Holy Spirit is filling us with His joy and power we know that this is not very different to us getting drunk from alcohol. He loves to be filling us throughout the course of our day. His aim is: giving us joy and thereby empowering us as Christians.

We need to experience this way of being drunk. Here we do not misbehave though. The anointing of the oil goes together with the drinking of the wine. Both represent the power of the Holy Spirit. In the above-mentioned scripture one could very clearly accept the fact that the psalmist is writing about wine in the spiritual sense, when he says: "my cup overflows." So his joy is complete.

This is why the pots standing at the bottom of the river are filled and the rest of the water flows over their tops, meters above the pots themselves.

Now, the pots floating on the surface of the water are filled only partially. This signifies believers when their blessings come at the moment when they are beginning to be filled by the Holy Spirit. The lives of these precious believers are being touched and changed by God in a good way, but they are tossed this way and that way, by various doctrines concerning the work of the Holy Spirit. This signifies the current of the water in the river as it tosses the pots around and so they cannot be filled completely.

This is why, at the moment when Christians step into the River of God, the power of the anointing touches them physically and they are changed on the inside. Suddenly though, some of them might find that the conflict in their lives increases. They now have new challenges to overcome.

1.b. The second part of the vision showed me where the vision actually begins: The pots at the bottom of the river were not filled in the same manner as those on the surface were filled. Those at the bottom are filled and completely covered by the river, which means that they were placed in the river when they were already full, so that they sank to the bottom quickly. Here they are fully submitted to the power of the river.

In a similar sense, believers are to be completely filled with the Holy Spirit and be totally submitted to Him. Then they move under His control.

These believers are obedient to the word of God and follow His instructions. There is a desire to please the Lord within them and He blesses them for their obedience. They do what the Lord says, they go where He sends. They respond with the same type of obedience which Abraham showed, when he had to offer his only son as a sacrifice to God.

Abraham had the blessing of God upon his life long before then, because he was obedient to God: Genesis 12 verses 2 and 3. Verse 2: "I will make you into a great nation and I will bless you; I will make your name great, and you will be a blessing." Verse 3: "I will bless those who bless you and whoever curses you I will curse; and all peoples on earth will be blessed through you!" There should be no questions asked and no reluctance, because nothing should take precedence over God's desire, His will, love and instruction.

The pots on the surface of the river symbolize those people who earnestly desire to be to be in the river, but they tried this by stepping into the river without being filled by the Holy Spirit. They want to have the miracles and the blessings, without being obedient to God and without making any sacrifices. They don't like letting go of sin in their lives. Since the river is so powerful, they do experience the Holy Spirit, but because they are not mature in the Lord, they later face conflict which they cannot handle. They find that they are morally unstable: tossed to and fro by various trials. They also experience loss of faith and hope.

These believers were receiving the gift of the Holy Spirit, but their eyes (spiritually), have not beheld the face of the Giver. They do not know the Giver, because they have not spent time in His presence. They have not learned to know his voice and to experience and enjoy his presence inwardly, because this comes after much devotion and with deeply seeking of his face. Only when He has prepared the believer, will they be able to "stand" as a witness of His power and love. So these people run after miracle services only to partake of and behold the Wonders, but they themselves are not mature Christians. They do not find it necessary to connect with God.

It is in His presence where we must first be filled with Him: his nature, character and love. Then we can easily act with obedience.

CHAPTER TWO

The Source

The second part of the vision in chapter one shows us how the other collection of pots was filled (the ones which were at the bottom of the river and which are standing firm).

These pots were standing at the bottom of a fountain. They remained there at the fountain, completely subjected to the flow of the water, until they were filled to the brim.

Then they were lifted by the hand of the Creator of the fountain, placed carefully inside the river and without much struggle, sank rapidly to the bottom. These vessels are then immovable and thus at complete rest.

When we look up to the Creator of this fountain, we see that the one who carries the pots to the river and allows them to sink to the bottom, is the one whom we have to behold even before we see the fountain itself. When we start with the enjoying of the gift, before we know the giver of it, we will suffer lots of confusion, instability and doubt in our Christian lives.

By the time we finally see the Giver for who He truly is (the Creator), we are almost overwhelmed by strife. It is therefore important to know that we cannot cease from strife merely by struggling with our problems on our own, because then we are at the wrong end of receiving from the Lord.

When we look up to see the face of the Giver we do so, because we see the source of the gift. We look up because we then realize that He is high above us and we need to humble ourselves before His majesty. As we look up to Him we worship and adore Him. At the same time also (because our focus is elevated), we see the source of the fountain, which is positioned at the front of the mountain, from where the flow of water comes. This is high up in the mountain, as I see it in my vision.

As we go to the bottom of the fountain we see the hand of the Giver. We are then below the fountain and He is above it.

So we look up to him and then—because we have come to him expectantly—he fills us up to the top and then places us in the river.

We need to look up and adore Jesus. We must learn to know his presence. This we can do best, only when we are alone with him. We need to have personal devotionals through Bible reading. We need our own praise and worship sessions at home when we pray and we should learn also—at certain times—how to be silent before the Lord and wait on the Holy Spirit for guidance.

 Read Isaiah 27 verse 13: "And in that day a great trumpet will sound. Those who were perishing in Assyria and those who were exiled in Egypt will come and worship the Lord on the holy mountain in Jerusalem." Isaiah 34 verse16: "Look into the scroll of the Lord and read: None of these will be missing, not one will lack her mate. For it is his mouth that has given the order, and his Spirit will gather them together." Also read Psalm 33 verse 1: "Sing joyfully to the Lord you righteous; it is fitting for the upright to praise him." Ecclesiastes 9 verse 17: "The quiet words of the wise are more to be heeded than the shouts of a ruler of fools."

1 Thessalonians 4 verse 11: "Make it your ambition to lead a quiet life, to mind your own business and to work with your hands, just as we told you," verse 12: "so that your daily life may win the respect of outsiders and so that you will not be dependent on anybody."

When a sense of God's presence seems slow to come it might be because we are not yet ready. We may have to remain at his feet while he prepares us for his presence. We need to pray and study his word while waiting on him. There might even be some sin we need to confess of before Him. Then suddenly, he blesses us with his presence. Here he fills us up and places us at the bottom of the river, where the fullness of his power is. Where not our will, but his resides continuously and in his peace.

Isaiah 32 verse 18: "My people will live in peaceful dwelling places, in secure homes, in undisturbed places of rest." Philippians 4 verse 7: "And the peace of God, which transcends all understanding, will guard your hearts and your minds in Christ Jesus." Also read 2 Peter 3 verse 13: "But in keeping with his promise we are looking forward to a new heaven and a new earth, the home of righteousness." Verse 14: "So then, dear friends, since you are looking forward to this, make every effort to be found spotless, blameless and at peace with him."

Also read John 6 verse 53: "Jesus said to them, I tell you the truth, unless you eat the flesh of the Son of man and drink his blood, you have no life in you." The life of Christ the giver and the lover comes from this fountain: John 6 verse 63: "The Spirit gives life; the flesh counts for nothing. The words I have spoken to you are spirit and they are life." This life is the spirit of God which flows as life, in the same way as the fountain does.

Thus we are already filled with the Holy Spirit at the time when we go into the river and we can trust that we move with Him, because we are one with him.

We cannot give ourselves over to flow in the manifestation of the Holy Spirit, when we do not have the guidance of Christ. This we gain through the intimacy of prayer, praise, reading of his word and by being quiet before him. When we do this, we find that nothing is alien to us. We are not shocked, neither do we shock or hurt anybody else. 1 Corinthians 10 verse 32: "Do not cause anyone to stumble, whether Jews, Greeks or the Church of God—verse 33: even as I try to please everybody in every way. For I am not seeking my own good, but the good of many so that they may be saved."

When we are already filled with the Holy Spirit we feel as refreshed as if we are new and we can receive instructions from Him as a result. We are with him in us, so we see things through his eyes. In this manner we become part of the miracles and we are not mere spectators.

CHAPTER THREE

Deliverance

Again in my local church, I once saw somebody in the spiritual sense, while looking at him in the natural. I was surprised by this, because I saw a giant lizard (Komodo dragon), draped around his shoulders. The creature had sly, evasive eyes; occasionally peering at me.

At first I did not know what to make of this, since this brother was a prominent pastor in the church. So I tried to forget what I saw.

At home later, this image remained with me, until I was compelled to ask the Lord about it.

The fact that this beast-like creature was on the shoulders of a highly anointed man of God, showed me that it was something which was definitely intending to interfere with the man's powerful anointing.

I realized in my spirit, that if this was interpreted in a spiritual sense, then this creature certainly represented a spirit of envy, which wanted to oppress and hinder the anointing of the brother. The lizard represented somebody who was seriously jealous of this man's anointing. For this to work it had to come from a fellow believer, unfortunately.

Usually it is somebody standing right next to us in these instances. They are not over on the enemy's side, although they are being tempted to sin. They cause so much pain because they cannot possibly miss their mark. The eyes of the beast I saw held lots of envy.

Why is jealousy so effective in oppressing a believer? Is God's grace not enough to prevent this?

This is however, the reason why Jesus commanded us to love one another, in order to be true disciples of His and to be known as such. Otherwise we will seriously hamper one another's growth, because it is within our power to do so.

It is important for us therefore, to examine ourselves and not to become envious of one another so that, when we sense a yoke like this on a fellow believer, we should love and relieve them, because we are as a mirror to them. They can feel the weight of something on them, but because it is around their shoulders, they would need a mirror to see exactly what it was. We should be true mirrors to one another and this can only come through love.

Read Song of Solomon 8 verses 6 and 7. Verse 6: "Place me like a seal over your heart, like a seal on your arm; for love is as strong as death, its jealousy unyielding as the grave. It burns like blazing fire, like a mighty flame." Verse 7: "Many waters cannot quench love; rivers cannot wash it away. If one were to give all the wealth of his house for love, it will be utterly scorned."

Also read Ezekiel 8 verse 3 to 18. Verse 3: "He stretched out what looked like a hand and took me by the hair of my head. The Spirit lifted me up between earth and heaven and in visions of God he took me to Jerusalem, to the entrance to the north gate of the inner court, where the idol that provokes to jealousy stood." Verse 4: "And there before me was the glory of the God of Israel, as in the vision I had seen in the plain." Verse 5: "Then he said to me, "Son of man, look toward the north." So I looked, and in the entrance north of the gate of the altar I saw this idol of jealousy." Verse 6: "And he said to me, "Son of man do you see what they are doing—the utterly detestable things the house of Israel is doing here, things that will drive me far from my sanctuary? But you will see things that are even more detestable." Verse 7: "Then he brought me to the entrance to the court. I looked, and saw a hole in the wall." Verse 8: "He said to me, "Son of man now dig into the wall." So I dug into the wall and saw a doorway there." Verse 9: "And he said to me, "Go in and see the wicked and detestable things they are doing here." Verse 10: "So I went in and looked and I saw portrayed all over the walls all kinds of crawling things and detestable animals and all of the idols of the house of Israel." Verse 11: "In front of them stood seventy elders of the house of Israel, and Jaazaniah son of Shaphan was standing among them. Each had a censer in his hand, and a fragrant cloud of incense was rising." Verse 12: "He said to me, "Son of man, have you seen what the elders of the house of Israel are doing in the darkness, each at the shrine of his own idol? They say, 'The Lord does not see us; the Lord has forsaken the land.' " Verse 13: "Again, he said, "You will see them doing things that are even more detestable." Verse 14: "Then he brought me to the entrance to the north gate of the house of the Lord, and I saw women sitting there, mourning for Tamuuz." Verse 15: "He said to me, "Do you see this, son of man? You will see things that are even more detestable than this." Verse 16: "He then brought me into the inner court of the house of the Lord, and there at the entrance to the temple, between the portico and the altar, were about twenty-five men. With their backs toward the temple of the Lord and their faces toward the east, they were bowing down to the sun in the east." Verse 17: "He said to me, "Have you seen this son of man? Is it a trivial matter for the house of Judah to do the detestable things they are doing here? Must they also fill the land with violence and continually provoke me to anger? Look at them putting the branch to their nose!" Verse 18: "Therefore I will deal with them in anger; I will not look on them with pity or spare them. Although they shout in my ears, I will not listen to them."

Here the house of Judah represents the Church of today: those already in the kingdom; the redeemed. In verse 3 we see the "image" or idol—which causes jealousy and which is a 50 centimeters sized lizard in my vision. The envious person would then simply carry on and remain in their state of envy.

In the same arena occupied by the image of jealousy, was the glory of the Lord: verse 4. So it can happen in the presence of the Lord and in church. In verse 5 we see the image of jealousy at the very gate of the altar. In verse 10 we see all the other abominable things which can happen right in the house of God and with the presence of his glory right there. Here we see those deeds portrayed as beasts as well.

So, the abominations could not erase the presence of the Lord from His house, but neither did the wrong-doing stop in the Lord's house. In verse 18 we see that God does not turn a blind eye to these dealings. In his time he will set things right.

Also, in the spiritual vision of the brother in church, I later saw (about two weeks later), that behind him stood a very large angel of protection. You see, we might cause one another to be oppressed, but God, in his greatness, provides for the better outcome of the matter, so that the person under attack will not in the end be defeated, though at times they might feel so and thus not be as active in ministry as they should be; they would lack their zeal and their "fire".

The angel is about ten times the size of the beast. He stands behind the believer so that; should the believer fall, he will fall backwards into the arms of God's grace, which here comes in the form of an angel. He will not even touch the ground in defeat.

Envy, however subtle, is displeasing to God, because therein lies the seed for doing every conceivable form of evil. So then, the very seed of it must be destroyed: Find out why you feel inadequate, because that is the cause for your feelings of envy. It may stem from something somebody said to you years ago, or a past experience of failure which you did not deal with at the time. Examine yourself in the presence of the Lord. Let Him heal you.

Envy might seem insignificant to the one holding it in their heart, but God does not want that kind of oppression on one of his children. He wants us all to move freely within our gifts and our anointing. He has so many dimensions of every gift or virtue to give us. There is more than enough for all of us. Why envy a person carrying a bucket of sea water, when there is an entire ocean only a few meters ahead? It is available to all who have need of it.

Because of its redemptive power, we can apply the blood of Jesus in this situation. Through the blood of Jesus, we can anoint any person's shoulders as his or her seat of power in God, so that envy; curses and hatred, have little effect on them. From then onwards they can be powerful in their ministry. We have to show them our love and concern.

So the oppressive spirit was rebuked by the brother and myself. I prayed and he agreed. We commanded it to stay away from him. If we do not take our authority in these matters, we will continue to suffer under the Devourer, as well as under one another. Spiritual warfare is very important. Do it with love for the person, but be aggressive and authoritative towards the oppressing spirit. We all need to be effective in ministry and move with power. Do not pamper the wicked spirit; address it with authority.

When I saw this pastor again a couple of weeks later, I could see the purpose of his ministry before him (in the spirit). In a vision, I saw his congregation in the form of sheep.

The sheep had wedding rings in their mouths. On top of each ring was a ruby stone as a decoration. To me this signified the marriage between the Church and Jesus (the rings), through his blood; as signified by the red color of the rubies.

This shepherd then blows on a trumpet to gather his flock and then shares messages from God with them. So here his prophetic ministry is seen as a form of essential inspiration for the flock under him.

The scene of the sheep bringing the rings as an offering to their leader (pastor), is a sign of them reconciling with him. His prophetic ministry can thus only bring him closer to the fuller glory of God, as he grows closer to his congregation. Revelations 17 verse 12: "The ten horns you saw are ten kings who have not yet received a kingdom, but who for one hour will receive authority as kings along with the beast." Verse 13: "They have one purpose and will give their power and authority to the beast." Verse 14: "They will make war against the Lamb, but the Lamb will overcome them because he is Lord of lords and King of kings—and with him will be his called, chosen and faithful followers."

This beast here portrayed is given its power. It is powerless on its own. So we must not give power to a seed of envy. Let it go away quickly. Verse 14 says: "they that are called are chosen and faithful. They move with Christ, the Lamb of God." The spirit of envy can drive you to do things which are harmful towards another person. So do not entertain it for a minute, because the Lord takes care of the faithful.

As a further form of encouragement, we must sometimes run and seek our refuge in the Lord, at times when we see that we are under a yoke (by looking into a spiritual mirror). Perhaps we feel spiritually weary or deflated, but we do not realize that it is a yoke. This can also occur when we give out too much and do not wait to receive.

We should never be too proud to receive. Even a child can pray for us and minister to us. So when the oppressive feeling comes we need to run for shelter at times. Isaiah 66 verse 13: "As a mother comforts her child, so will I comfort you; and you will be comforted over Jerusalem." Verse 14: "When you see this, your heart will rejoice and you will flourish like grass; the hand of the Lord will be made known to his servants, but his fury will be shown to his foes."

Here we can see the motherly nature of God, as he comforts us by giving us rest and by healing our bruises. Verse 14 says that in this care you will be newly inspired with joy. This joy surges through the body, anointing every part of us. Our bones will no longer be spiritually weary. Usually a lack of interest in the things of God leads to "spiritually aching bones". Maybe the bones are dry and that is why they ache. Sometimes we suffer a big loss in life and "our bones become dry". So then they do need the nourishing of the Holy Spirit. In this way God rewards those who serve Him.

We cannot be anointed, yet fail to serve. Revelation 17 verse 14 says those who are called are also chosen and faithful. Therefore they qualify because God qualifies them. They are also faithful in character and so achieve favor in Christ. Thus then, they deal with their spiritually aching bones. So the Lord loves them for their faithfulness.

Since God is faithful in everything, we could consider being more like him. We need to be trustworthy, or we are not his servants. In the following scripture we see how God can defend himself: Isaiah 66 verse 15: "See, the Lord is coming with fire and his chariots are like a whirlwind; he will bring down his anger with fury and his rebuke with flames of fire." Verse 16: "For with fire and with his sword the Lord will execute judgment upon all men, and many will be those slain by the Lord." Verse 17: "Those who consecrate and purify themselves to go into the gardens, following the one in the midst of those who eat the flesh of pigs and rats and other abominable things—they will meet their end together, declares the Lord." Verse 18: "And I, because of their actions and their imaginations, am about to come and gather all nations and tongues, and they will come and see my glory." Verse 19: "I will set a sign among them, and I will send some of those who survive to the nations—to Tarshish, to the Libyans and Lydians, to Tubal and Greece, and to the distant Islands that have not heard of my fame or seen my glory. They will proclaim my glory among the nations." Verse 20: "And they will bring all your brothers, from all the nations, to my holy mountain in Jerusalem as an offering to the Lord—on horses, in chariots and wagons, and on mules and camels," says the Lord. "They will bring them, as the Israelites bring their grain offerings, to the temple of the Lord in ceremonially clean vessels." Verse 21: "And I will select some of them also to be priests and Levites, says the Lord." Verse 22: "As the new heavens and the new earth that I make will endure before me, declares the Lord, so will your name and descendants endure." Verse 23: "From one New Moon to another and from one Sabbath to another, all mankind will come and bow down before me, says the Lord." Verse 24: "And they will go out and look upon the dead bodies of those who rebelled against me; their worm will not die, nor will their fire be quenched, and they will be loathsome to all mankind."

His glory is bigger than anything else. He will reveal his glory in all such circumstances. Also in the circumstances of your life.

When I have a vision of Jesus as he sits in glory, in heaven, I often see him with a crown on his head and the crown is not always the same. Sometimes it has multicolored lights inside it. It is often decorated with all kinds of precious stones and at other times it just radiates lights of many colors. At times his glory is also in the form of a halo.

The Lord's glory in heaven is represented by the ever present light there. I know this due to having had some near death experiences; when I had been out of my physical body for a certain amount of time. Here the light feels like the most powerful force in heaven. It is filled with love and peace. The loves goes right through the body of a human being. It embraces everything. It is the greatest force I have ever experienced and it is beautiful beyond measure. It is very bright, but in a comfortable way and it fills a person with indescribable joy.

In heaven one feels light; weightless. This makes one feel like jumping without end. One can jump forever, because of the immense joy filling one's entire being.

This then, is how important and powerful the glory of God is. It has the power to change any force on earth. **So there should never be any need to worry about whether God will be able to help you out of your problems. He is God Almighty.**

CHAPTER FOUR

Servitude

Another beautiful way of serving a fellow believer is to share the inspirational visions or dreams we have of them; when the Lord gives these to us. He wouldn't give them to us if the people, or person involved, did not need help.

Concerning one specific believer the Lord showed me the following: I saw the brother in Christ kneeling in front of a small dam filled with what looked like red wine. This immediately reminded me that the Lord likened the wine to his blood shed on the cross, when he held the Last Supper with his disciples.

At the opposite end of the dam, the Lord Jesus stood with arms outstretched, in the form of a blessing towards the brother.

On the surface of this dam was a string of pearls in the form of a crown.

After this I saw the Lord majestically up in the air and rising slowly, with the sun behind him. The sun was surrounding him in a glorious light. His arms were still outstretched as a blessing. With the blessing he gives, he is also closing his eyes in prayer.

Interpretation

The dam appears to be the secret place where this believer meets with the Lord when he prays. The crown of pearls appears to me to be his reward after trials in his life. A pearl is formed through the discomfort of the oyster, as liquid secretions pile up slowly in layers and harden; tiny drops at a time, in order to cover and soothe a point of irritation, which is caused by a grain on the body of the oyster, over a lengthy period of time. This signifies patience and longsuffering. Thus the secretions form the beautiful pearl, inside the shell. It is a slow and uncomfortable process, resulting in great beauty.

Hebrews 12 verse 11: "No discipline seems pleasant at the time of trial. It is painful. Later on, however, it produces a harvest of righteousness and peace for those who have been trained by it." 1 Timothy 1 verse 16: "But for that very reason I was shown mercy so that in me, the worst of sinners, Christ Jesus might display his unlimited patience as an example for those who would believe on him and receive eternal life."

So this brother has an entire collection of pearls in the form of a crown. This signifies his crown of life.

At this point the Lord rises up and is glorified above the brother and his circumstances (those things which merely seek to bog us down, but on which we often concentrate all of our efforts). At the same time the Lord is praying for this brother to the Father, as we see in John 17 verse 9: "I pray for them, I am not praying for the world, but for those you have given me, for they are yours." Verse 10: "All I have is yours, and all you have is mine. And glory has come to me through them." Verse 11: "I will remain in the world no longer, but they are still in the world, and I am coming to you. Holy Father, protect them by the power of your name—the name you gave me—so that they may be one as we are one." Verse 12: "While I was with them, I protected them and kept them safe by that name you gave me. None has been lost except the one doomed to destruction so that Scripture may be fulfilled." Verse 13: "I am coming to you now, but I say these things while I am still in the world, so that they may have the full measure of my joy within them." Verse 14: "I have given them your word and the world has hated them, for they are not of the world any more than I am of the world." Verse 15: "My prayer is not that you take them out of the world but that you protect them from the evil one." Verse 16: "They are not of the world, even as I am not of it." Verse 17: "Sanctify them by the truth; your word is truth." Verse 18: "As you have sent me into the world, I have sent them into the world." Verse 19: "For them I sanctify myself, that they too may be truly sanctified." Verse 20: "My prayer is not for them alone. I pray also for those who will believe in me through their message," verse 21: "that all of them may be one, Father, just as you are in me and I am in you. May they also be in us so that the world may believe that you have sent me." Verse 22: "I have given them the glory that you gave me, that they may be one as we are one." Verse 23: "I in them and you in me. May they be brought to complete unity to let the world know that you have sent me and have loved them even as you have loved me." Verse 24: "Father, I want those you have given me to be with me where I am, and to see my glory, the glory you have given me because you loved me before the creation of the world." Verse 25: "Righteous Father, though the world does not know you, I know you, and they know that you have sent me." Verse 26: "I have made you known to them, and will continue to make you known in order that the love you have for me may be in them and that I myself may be in them."

In conclusion: I finally had a vision of this brother with glorious pink fumes (like a cloud) mingled with golden stars, above his head, resembling a crown of glory.

Also, at this time the picture of an elderly, wise-looking man came to me in a vision. This happened to me a few times afterwards and really did fascinate me each time it happened. His hair was long and white. He was seated by the mountain-side, holding a staff like a shepherd. His eyes looked intense and stern, but they also held a look of intense love. Those are the eyes which see everything. I think this is a spiritual personification of God the Father, although he is one with the son. I see them both (individually though), but the one is in the other.

CHAPTER FIVE

The River in the book of Ezekiel

The following scripture is a specific example of the river of God's promise and His presence; for us to enjoy. Ezekiel 47 verse 1: "The man brought me back to the entrance of the temple, and I saw water coming out from under the threshold of the temple toward the east (for the temple faced east). The water was coming down from under the south side of the temple, south of the altar." Verse 2: "He then brought me out through the north gate and led me around the outside to the outer gate facing east, and the water was flowing from the south side." Verse 3: "As the man went eastward with a measuring line in his hand, he measured off a thousand cubits and then led me through water that was ankle-deep." Verse 4: "He measured off another thousand cubits and led me through water that was knee-deep. He measured off another thousand and led me through water that was up to the waist." Verse 5: "He measured off another thousand, but now it was a river that I could not cross, because the water had risen and was deep enough to swim in—a river that no one could cross." Verse 6: He asked me, " Son of man, do you see this?" Then he led me back to the bank of the river." Verse 7: "When I arrived there, I saw a great number of trees on each side of the river." Verse 8: "He said to me, "This water flows toward the eastern region and goes down into the Arabah, where it enters the Sea. When it empties into the Sea, the water there becomes fresh." Verse 9: "Swarms of living creatures will live wherever the river flows. There will be large numbers of fish, because this water flows there and makes the salt water fresh; so where the river flows everything will live." Verse 10: "Fishermen will stand along the shore; from En Gedi to En Eglaim there will be places for spreading nets. The fish will be of many kinds—like the fish of the Great Sea." Verse 11: But the swarms and marshes will not become fresh; they will be left for salt." Verse 12: "Fruit trees of all kinds will grow on both banks of the river. Their leaves will not wither, nor will their fruit fail. Every month they will bear, because the water from the sanctuary flows to them. Their fruit will serve for food and their leaves for healing."

Now, in the spiritual sense, if we place ourselves in this picture, we see the river beginning to make contact at our feet, as we step into it and we realize that this is a rather significant point, because it is the most important point of contact (we overcome our fear). If we as believers step into the river of God for the first time, the initial contact will be a shock to the system, just as the water shocks the physical body when one tentatively places one's feet into the cold water of a river or a swimming pool.

As a result of our getting touched by the Spirit of God, when we step into God's river, we might find that we do things which we never thought possible. We may have our first vision, or speak in an unknown tongue (spiritual language) and we might later discover that we have the gift to heal the sick. Other spiritual gifts may follow as long as we remain in the River.

Going deeper, the water reaches our knees. In the spiritual realm we also manifest our growth here. We may realize that we have received a command from God and then we have to decide whether or not we are going to obey it. So we become more active in ministry. We are not caught completely by surprise when the Holy Spirit touches us and spiritual things begin to make more sense to us.

So we are more committed to the water. We are more accustomed to its ebb and flow. It is becoming a familiar sensation. With this may come the desire to learn more, but we might also decide to draw back, because of a feeling of getting too much of a "new thing". This might be because of peer group pressure for the young, or religious pressure for those who are traditionally accustomed to a more "dignified" and structured form of worship.

If we choose to move deeper into the river—to knee deep level—we also choose to know more about God. We want more of His touch and we desire clear instruction from Him. We are excited and eager to obey. We love the flow of the Holy Spirit.

With obedience here at this point comes an increase of the anointing upon our lives. People notice our growth and this is exciting. So we want to do more in the spiritual realm. We endeavor to understand our spiritual gifts better.

Reaching this point may vary from one Christian to another, depending upon various factors such as: background in faith; level of faith and sincerity during worship.

The next stage is when the water of the river reaches our waists. We have gone in deeper and become even more committed to the Holy Spirit's control. We are also now more sensitive than at the other stages of flowing in the Spirit. We learn to hear the voice of the Lord.

We also set ourselves apart for a time with the Father; seeking His face while meditating upon His Word and while soaking in His presence during worship.

With the water of the river at your waist level you are now fully committed to swim. You are ready to respond to whatever you believe the Lord to be saying through His Spirit, as He interprets His word to you, or gives you a vision. You will go where He sends you. You can feel the power of the river and it is ready to sweep you off into its current. Your will should become fully submitted to His and you will find yourself also enjoying the surge of His power, as it fills you. Then you are not only halfway in. You are completely submitted to Him and ready to follow His instruction without the slightest hesitation.

Verses 5 and 6 mention that the river rises to a level where one has to swim, but the river is so wide that it is not possible to cross it.

In the spiritual sense here we are in obedience and we are experiencing the effects, as well as the consequences of acting out of obedience. We cannot get away from this because, once an action has been carried out, one must be prepared both for its effect and its results.

The consequences of the actions we consider to be divine may vary. When serving fellow believers for example, one finds that some will be ecstatic about the mere fact that God cares about them. On the other hand, others are mainly conscious of the fact that they should be protecting themselves and they will not readily welcome any kind of spiritual input into their lives. They might also consider it to be an invasion of their privacy.

We therefore should remember that during instances where we have a word of knowledge or wisdom for somebody, we should be mindful of the fact that love and prophesy is for good and inspiration. Anything that is contrary to this can be considered to possess an ill motive and is therefore not from the Lord. He does not curse us. Jesus took away curses when He was on the cross. So we cannot tell a brother or sister in Christ that they are cursed, or that they are doomed to loss or failure.

So, when folk reject the message we share, we should be prepared to live with that response. The river has its own life. We are a part of the flow of the river when we are carried by its current. We are not the essence of the river, so we should not take the rejection personally. It is God doing His work in that particular person. We are merely the tools he uses when we are available. So then, instead of hurting from our disappointment, we should be eagerly awaiting his next command, with love for him and forgiveness towards the person who lacks understanding.

If a person refuses any form of prophesy whatsoever, it is very important to respect their wishes and to just pray for them on your own instead.

The overriding factor here is that we should experience the joy of the river. We can only be joyful, because we have ventured into the river of our own compulsion. We would expect fear of the power of the river only if somebody pushed us in. For example: if someone wants to force us to pray in tongues. We do know however, that God always invites us to try him and to taste his goodness. He does not force us into the river.

So, fear should not be part of our flow in the river. Otherwise we would not be floating or swimming. We would be spluttering spiritually. From verse 7 we see that the river is fruitful, because it causes the lush growth of trees, up until verse 12. So this river can feed people with fish and fruit and at the same time it also provides healing, because of the leaves of the fruit trees. This is very much the same with our spiritual river. We are fed spiritually so that we can grow and our spiritual river—the Holy Spirit—also heals our bodies and our souls. So we cannot grow if we are unwilling to be in the river.

Concerning the gift of prophesy, we should read 1 Corinthians 14 verse 29: "Two or three prophets should speak, and the others should weigh carefully what is said." Verse 30: "And if a revelation comes to someone who is sitting down, the first speaker should stop." Verse 31: "For you can all prophesy in turn so that everyone may be instructed and encouraged." Verse 32: "The spirits of prophets are subject to the control of prophets." Verse 33: "For God is not a God of disorder but of peace."

Here we have the spiritual food and growth through the Holy Spirit, as it is portrayed in the river from the scripture. We are fed by prophesy as well as the Word.

Another form of feeding is explained in Malachi 3 verse 10: "Bring the whole tithe into the storehouse, that there may be food in my house. Test me in this, says the Lord Almighty, and see if I will not throw open the floodgates of heaven and pour out so much blessing that you will not have enough room for it." Here we see that God is interested in our physical feeding and He wants to bless us spiritually as well. We do feed in his house spiritually. The food referred to in the scripture is the provision which the Church makes for those who are serving in the Church; therefore "dwelling" in the Lord's house.

Every house needs food in it and so also does the Lord's house. The food here assumes the form of financial provision. We feed spiritually, therefore we should give of our finances, in order that those who serve in the Lord's house can feed physically. We do this with the promise of a great blessing from the Lord for our obedience. So in the end, we are actually investing in ourselves when we pay our tithes. We do not suffer loss, because God keeps His promises.

Part 2
Devotion

Dedicated to my brother, James Gerald Lambert: 1957–1987. We were very close and I love you, always.

CHAPTER SIX

His word

The word of God is as a sword to us, so that we will be able to engage in spiritual warfare.

In Hebrews 4 verse 12 we learn that the word of God is sharper than any double-edged sword. When a sword has two edges we know that it cuts on both sides. This would also imply that at some point between the edges, the sword must be flat, or curved, thus totally safe to the touch. If we used this section to strike the enemy in battle, it would not produce fatal results. This part can actually stroke the enemy gently, not leaving even a scar. Using a weapon in this way does not convey a serious message. It can even be mistaken as an attempt towards a joke. So when we follow the Word we should follow it all the way and not halfway, because then we end up in the middle. This is the point where we compromise and this is also where we are misled and fall into sin, thereby making a mockery of God's word.

The word "battle" indicates a fight between two opposing sides (people who do not agree with one another). So it is but natural to expect your opposition to also have weapons. The situation is potentially fatal to those who are unskilled in fighting (not being equipped with knowledge or wisdom to the required degree). Ezekiel 33 verse 32: "Indeed, to them you are nothing more than one who sings love songs with a beautiful voice and plays an instrument well, for they hear your words but do not put them into practice." Also Hebrews 5 verse 13: "Anyone who lives on milk, being still an infant, is not acquainted with the teaching about righteousness." Verse 14: "But solid food is for the mature, who by constant use have trained themselves to distinguish good from evil."

A sword can be placed into anyone's hands. Thus we know and understand that anyone can hold the Bible in their hands, but they could be led by all kinds of agendas. The Word can be used for various purposes. Sadly, some purposes are not to honor God only. The aim in sharing the Word should be to glorify God and to see His purpose fulfilled. Not to manipulate Him and not to glorify ourselves.

If we use our swords without sufficient training and without the guidance of the Expert, we could wind up just tickling or stroking the enemy whom we are trying to remove from our lives and from the lives of others.

So then, when we next see the person we have ministered to, they would not recall the impact, or the content of our message, because we were mediocre in our delivery of it. In order for us to fight a battle, the Lord of the battle should train us and therefore we must look to him and not forget to focus on him, because our spiritual lives depend on this. The only other way out is to not go to battle at all, which is tragic from the outset, because that would mean that the soldier has been "killed" before going to battle. Therefore he or she has no experience of fighting. This means that they gave up when they faced their first trial as a Christian, because they told themselves that they were too weak to stand up for their faith.

In battle you can either move forwards or backwards. Otherwise you are stagnating and this state of being cannot last for long. In the spiritual context this means that you cannot simply remain inactive in battle. That would mean that you are either not a soldier at all, or that you are not alive. As a growing Christian you will be engaged in spiritual battles.

In the Bible the Lord says that the battle is his: Read Hebrews 10 verse 30. Therefore we are not alone in our fight. He is actually fighting for us. Our fight is against temptation. So we need to know how to use the Word, in order to stand firm against various temptations. We learn this by faithfully studying the Bible. Also, if there is anything we need in our lives, all we need to do is to tell the Lord about it and he will fight for us to achieve it. We need to rest in Him, just as little children trust that their parents will do right by them.

2 Samuel 22 verse 29: "You are my lamp, O Lord; the Lord turns my darkness into light." Verse 30: "With your help I can advance against a troop, with my God I can scale a wall." Verse 31: "As for my God, his way is perfect; the word of the Lord is flawless. He is a shield for all who take refuge in him." Verse 32: "For who is God besides the Lord? And who is the Rock except our God?" Verse 33: "It is God who arms me with strength and makes my way perfect." Verse 34: "He makes my feet like the feet of a deer; he enables me to stand on the heights." Verse 35: "He trains my hands for battle; my arms can bend a bow of bronze." Verse 36: "You give me your shield of victory; you stoop down to make me great." Verse 37: "You broaden the path beneath me, so that my ankles do not turn." Verse 38: "I pursued my enemies and crushed them; I did not turn back till they were destroyed." Verse 39: "I crushed them completely, and they could not rise; they fell beneath my feet." Verse 40: "You armed me with strength for battle; you made my adversaries bow at my feet." Verse 41: "You made my enemies turn their backs in flight, and I destroyed my foes." Verse 42: "They cried for help, but there was no one to save them—to the Lord, but he did not answer." Verse 43: "I beat them as fine as the dust of the earth; I pounded and trampled them like mud in the streets." Verse 44: "You have delivered me from the attacks of my people; you have preserved me as the head of nations. People I did not know are subject to me," verse 45: "and foreigners come cringing to me; as soon as they hear me, they obey me." Verse 46: "They all lose heart; they come trembling from their strongholds." Verse 47: "The Lord lives! Praise be to my Rock! Exalted be God, the Rock, my Savior!" Verse 48: "He is the God who avenges me, who puts the nations under me," Verse 49: "who sets me free from my enemies. You exalted me above my foes; from violent men you rescued me." Verse 50: "Therefore I will praise you, O

Lord, among the nations; I will sing praises to your name." Verse 51: "He gives his king great victories; he shows unfailing kindness to his anointed, to David and his descendants forever."

Isaiah 41 verse 8: "But you, O Israel, my servant, Jacob, whom I have chosen, you descendants of Abraham my friend," Verse 9: "I took you from the ends of the earth, from its farthest corners I called you. I said, 'you are my servant'; I have chosen you and have not rejected you." Verse 10: "So do not fear, for I am with you; do not be dismayed, for I am your God. I will strengthen you and help you; I will uphold you with my righteous right hand." Verse 11: "All who rage against you will surely be ashamed and disgraced; those who oppose you will be as nothing and perish." Verse 12: "Though you search for your enemies, you will not find them. Those who wage war against you will be as nothing at all." Verse 13: "For I am the Lord, your God, who takes hold of your right hand and says to you, Do not fear; I will help you." Verse 14: "Do not be afraid, O worm Jacob, O little Israel, for I myself will help you," declares the Lord, your Redeemer, the Holy One of Israel." Verse 15: "See, I will make you into a threshing sledge, new and sharp, with many teeth. You will thresh the mountains and crush them, and reduce the hills to chaff." Verse 16: "You will winnow them, the wind will pick them up, and a gale will blow them away. But you will rejoice in the Lord and glory in the Holy One of Israel." Verse 17: "The poor and needy search for water, but there is none; their tongues are parched with thirst. But I the Lord will answer them; I, the God of Israel, will not forsake them." Verse 18: "I will make rivers flow on barren heights, and springs within the valleys. I will turn the desert into pools of water, and the parched ground into springs." Verse 19: "I will put in the desert the cedar and the acasia, the myrtle and the olive. I will set pines in the wasteland, the fir and the cypress together," Verse 20: "so that people will see and know, may consider and understand, that the hand of the Lord has done this, that the Holy One of Israel has created it." Verse 21: "Present your case," says the Lord. Set forth your arguments," says Jacob's king."

In all the above statements we see how God wants to assist us in battle. Therefore we are not alone as we fight the enemy.

So place your hand in his with confidence and do not pay heed to any of the whisperings of the enemy who seeks to destroy you. You have your promises from God, so rejoice in them. Instead of fearing a negative outcome of your situation, trust that God has already won the victory on your behalf. Thank him for it and praise him every available moment of the day.

CHAPTER SEVEN

I
The fountain

As what I would consider to be an extension of the vision I had in Part 1: Dedication—the section which mentions the river of God—I later had a vision concerning an interesting fountain: I saw a wide stream coming down a mountainside, like a wall, in the form of a flood. At the bottom where it falls though, it forms a small dam and then from there it forms a narrow stream, which trickles off as a small fountain, down a hill and into an even tinier stream, some distance further along.

II
Spiritual Interpretation

At the beginning of a revival or any great new move of the Holy Spirit (the big wall of water), we experience blessings in the form of an overwhelming surge of life within us. As we continue with our Christian lives, but do not allow ourselves to be continually filled by the Holy Spirit, we experience less of that life-giving spring of joy in our lives and in our ministry.

We are less inspired and it seems as if the general toil of life draws away our anointing, inner healing and joy.

In another sense, the vision would also indicate the amount of believers during a revival: The believers come into the large stream of the fountain, at its beginning. Then the stream becomes more structured and fewer believers are in this stream. As the stream acquires even more direction it becomes somewhat narrower and therefore even fewer believers are swimming in this stream.

III
Reasons

1.a Most of us love the novelty stage of everything we value in life. So when we are first baptized in the Holy Spirit and filled with Him, we feel as if the joy could last forever. As time goes on though and we start missing Church services or prayer gatherings (because of other social commitments), this anointing on our lives becomes diluted and our joy starts to diminish. It is not revival time anymore, so it is difficult to motivate oneself. The revival time becomes a distant memory. So we just carry on and drag ourselves along, while anticipating the next church revival, which is perhaps only due in a year's time. And so the years pass on, until the day when we do not make it for the next revival.

1.b. The masses follow the direction of those in the lead. Each person can only look right ahead and not to the back, or way ahead at the leader. Focus is lost easily, because the people's attention shifts quickly to others and to the circumstances around them. So they seldom focus on the goal up ahead, which is the end post. Such people lose their personal direction easily, because they follow the more general ways and the directions of the crowd immediately surrounding them.

There is also lots of fun and intermingling in the large stream. So it is easy to become frivolous and therefore lose focus of one's personal goals.

IV
Advice

2.a. One should take great care to be a Christian who knows how to maintain their joy in the Lord. Go to church and prayer meetings regularly, but remember to also spend time on your own, seeking God's presence in prayer and worship at home. Grab a few moments aside and do it at work also, when you get a chance. Don't wait for a crisis to arise. Make it a habit for a healthy spiritual life.

2.b. Move away from the crowd. In the narrower stream there is less fun and there are many more moments of being alone. But being alone though, can also mean spending more meaningful quiet time with the Lord and this is where one's life really becomes structured as a believer. This is where you gain strength and grow.

3.a. For spiritual encouragement read 1 Peter 5 verse 4: "And when the Chief Shepherd appears, you will receive the crown of glory that will never fade away." Verse 5: "Young men, in the same way be submissive to those who are older. All of you, clothe yourselves with humility toward one another, because, God opposes the proud but gives grace to the humble." Verse 6: "Humble yourselves, therefore, under God's mighty hand, that he may lift you up in due time." Verse 7: "Cast all your anxiety on him because he cares for you." Verse 8: "Be self-controlled and alert. Your enemy the devil prowls around like a roaring lion looking for someone to devour." Verse 9: "Resist him, standing firm in the faith, because you know that your brothers throughout the world are undergoing the same kind of sufferings." Verse 10: "And the God of all grace, who called you to his eternal glory in Christ, after you have suffered a little while, will himself restore you and make you strong, firm and steadfast."

3.b. For more encouragement and fullness of joy read Hebrews 12 verses 2 to 14. Also read Matthew 5 Verses 11 and 12.

CHAPTER EIGHT

I
The Father's hand

When we walk with the Lord, with our hand in his—so we do not stumble or fall—we should keep our focus on him and not on everyone and everything around us. Otherwise we will be swaying and dangling every which way.

It is the same as when a father takes his child for a walk and the child is looking in all directions at everything around him or her. The child only looks at his or her father to ask for ice-cream or sweets (candy). This is when we take the Lord's hand of guidance for granted and only look to Him for our provision, wants and desires. Instead we should also enjoy just being with him; basking in his presence.

Read Numbers 11 verse 23; 2 Samuel 24 verse 14 and Nehemiah 2 verse 18.

II
The fire and the blood.

I once had a vision about red wine coming from the midst of a pile of rocks. This—in color—resembled the lava in a volcano.

I realized that a volcano reaches far and beyond its immediate area. Even where one cannot see the lava anymore, one cannot walk, because of the scalding heat.

For me the red wine signifies the blood of Jesus and in this instance we see that it can flow from the apparent barrenness of a few rocks and like a volcano, it reaches far beyond where it is visible. It even affects the feet of those who walk kilometers away, far from where it can be seen bubbling out like a fountain.

So the Blood can reach what may seem like spiritually barren people and areas of life even beyond what the human eye can see and what can be conceived by the mind. **Those we consider to be beyond all redemption can still be saved by the power of the Blood.**

A volcano is also very hot. It displays most extraordinarily high peaks in temperature. The effect of the blood of Jesus is just as powerful, because it is similar to a personal touch from God himself. Hebrews 12 verse 29 states: "our God is a consuming fire". A volcano is scalding in effect. There can be no doubt about that fact. The expression "consuming fire" also indicates that the fire takes complete control. It does not work in half measures. So also is the power of the Blood, because it saves completely. You can never be only halfway saved.

III
Grace

First event
I once looked up along the pavement of a busy part of town called Arcadia, in Pretoria. The Arcadia and adjacent

Sunnyside areas do not embrace a high level of morality. On this occasion I decided to look into the spiritual realm. What I saw amazed me, because I saw throngs of angels moving around very busily and quite fast. They seemed a whole lot more busy than the crowds of people and out-numbered them by about ten times.

People here would very seldom show up in a church, yet the Lord sheds his abundant love and grace upon them. They need it much more than the sober-minded, morally upright people out there; as seems apparent by the very large amount of angels here. Much more than around the more quiet and dignified areas.

Second event
Over a period of about two months: October to November in 1998, I had a series of visions about a Jakaranda tree (a tree with purple blossoms), standing in the middle of the parking area of the bottle store and a bar, which were close to where I lived. Round about the tree, on the ground, was a glorious pile of purple flowers and petals. The tree is like a throne in the middle of this purple splendor. John 1 verse 17: "For the law was given through Moses; grace and truth came through Jesus Christ." Romans 5 verse 20: "The law was added so that the trespass might increase. But where sin increased, grace increased all the more," Verse 21: "so that, just as sin reigned in death, so also grace might reign through righteousness, to bring eternal life through Jesus Christ our Lord."

So we see that where there is a low level of morality God does not turn away from those people. He gives them the chance to meet up with Him by giving them a lot of grace, because they might be ignorant about the love He has for them. Therefore they need time to hear the gospel and then they can see and understand that it is the better option for them.

I sense that this is what God wants us to know about faith. We should anticipate the glory of the future outcome of a situation even while we see it in its present dismal state. So the purple color in the vision stands for heavenly royalty, which can be the outcome for the people who visit the bar and the bottle store, when they have at last accepted Christ into their lives one beautiful day.

IV
Glory

At this point I would like to share one of the visions I regularly have of the Lord Jesus. In this vision he is portrayed in glory. I see him holding a staff in his hand and raising it up in the air like a shepherd and at the same time he is sitting upon waves of purple water up in the sky. Above him and around his head are tiny golden stars.

Here I can see Jesus glorified and as a caring shepherd at the same time. For me, the purple water signifies his royal glory as well as the current flow of the Holy Spirit in our lives. He is royalty, but he cares about the average person out there, because he wants to guide them as a shepherd.

The stars show me his anointing and his glory, all around his head. They portray his royalty like a crown. So our Shepherd is a King.

V
Encouragement

In our churches we need to be aware of the fact that we have to uplift one another's spirits through the power of the Holy Spirit. Of course we learn to do this by practicing in our homes with our loved ones first. If you are already feeling on top of the world, because you have encouraged your spouse and other loved ones at home, it would be natural to continue in this trend at church and at other places you go to. In this way we show that we love the Lord. John 15 verse 12: "My command is this: Love each other as I have loved you."

I shared this word with someone at church. This is somebody who is small in stature, but he is a strong leader in the church. I do not usually bring a word of encouragement to a man, nor do I counsel or lay hands on a member of the opposite sex, but there are exceptional cases like this.

What I said was: "If you are a person of small stature, remember that you can have a hand in determining your physical size. Not in height, but in weight. Largely it is God's idea for you to have the height which you end up with, eventually. In Jesus' eyes though, you have a spiritual size which is much larger and taller than you are in the natural." For some of us it can also be the other way around, unfortunately. So make him big in your eyes and one day you will be surprised to see how big he has made you. See him as very high and lifted up."

The outer shell means little. It is but a temporary dwelling. What matters is the size of your spirit inside of you. So we need to be humble and show forgiveness, love and mercy to those around us.

CHAPTER NINE

I
Obedience

It is often important to God that we cooperate when someone blesses us with a word of knowledge, combined with wisdom. It is wise though to know and trust the person before acting on anything received.

There was a brother and a sister in the Lord whom I knew and they were planning to get married, but they did not have much financial means. The Lord showed me a vision of the young man, where the Lord Jesus gives him corn and some gold coins. Then again I saw the brother on a mountainside with the Lord Jesus. The brother was kneeling by a waterfall. The water fell into a dam and in the dam there were fishes swimming. I knew then that the fishes were representing the souls which this young brother should reach.

The waterfall was the presence of God in which this brother had to abide. The dam represented his place of work, which was his mission field as portrayed by the fishes. There is also an act of planting a seed, as seen by the corn in his hand. So, as long as he plants a seed there is hope for him to catch the fishes one day. The corn can also be seen as bait for catching the fishes. The reward for planting and fishing would be the gold in his hand—this brother would receive the financial blessings represented by the gold coins.

This vision was for the brother to realize that his workplace (the seed planting and fishing) was his mission field. In this case he would be surprised with a financial reward. This does not imply that God rewards us with cash for reaping souls. It was a unique case for that particular time only, because there happened to be a financial need.

I received the following scripture to go with the prophesy: I Timothy 6 verses 17 to 19. In light of this I told the brother that I sensed that, through his sharing of the gospel in his place of employment, he would receive extra financial blessings upon his life.

As he later testified; this brother had work to do somewhere away from his jobsite one day and as he was preparing to return to the office, he suddenly realized that God wanted him to return and pray for the clients he had just been speaking to. He obeyed without questioning the Lord and the people were emotionally touched by his gesture, because he asked if he could pray for them. They really needed prayer for healing, more than anything else. And so someone was healed in their body at that time and they all came to know the Lord right there and then. Thereafter these people (who happened to be wealthy), offered him the gift of an all-expenses paid honeymoon, to any destination of his choice in the world. He was astounded and yes, felt truly blessed because of his act of obedience, on the spot, without delay.

II
The presence of God

When we are in the Lord's presence we are bathed into the Holy Spirit. This happens and inevitably results must follow.

In the beginning stage we seek healing from our deepest emotional wounds. We would often do a lot of weeping at this stage. Here His love does all the work in healing us inwardly.

The second stage is when we begin to manifest His presence physically: shaking; falling; etc. We also manifest verbally: speaking in tongues; prophesying; laughing; etc.

Thirdly we need to listen to the Lord and enquire about his will for us, concerning our calling and our personal lives. We need to get to know his voice and therefore hear when he is speaking to us. We discover our calling when we respond to needs.

During this period of being in God's presence regularly, we all need guidance from our prayer groups. We need lots of patience and God's perfect timing. When the time is right, the required result will occur.

We also need guidance from the pastors; prophets; evangelists and apostles in our churches, so that we can grow.

There can be a problem though, when we spend time being bathed into and being moved by the Holy Spirit and yet do not mature spiritually. We then never discover our gifts and thereby, our calling in ministry. We always manifest His touch, but never function in any ministry. To deal with this situation so that we can grow, we should read our Bibles faithfully and volunteer in ministry, in order to develop spiritually. As you volunteer in various ministries you will find the one that is right for you.

The presence of the Lord is also for filling up with joy and recharging on it regularly, so that the joy of the Lord can keep us strong. It is also there for us to learn from God: what it is that he wants to impact on us through his Holy Spirit; who teaches us things we would not know in the natural. When we do not do this, we might be using the Lord's presence and his power only as a momentary thrill.

This kind of indulgence (taking the Lord for granted) can lead to defeatism; boredom and a non-progressive Christian life, which includes the tragedy of never getting rid of familiar sin in our lives.

Read 2 Corinthians 1 verses 21 and 22; 2 Corinthians 12 verse 9; 1 Timothy 2 verses 5 to 7; Hebrews 3 verses 1 and 2 and Matthew 3 verse 11.

CHAPTER TEN

I
The Old church

On 15th November 1998 I had a vision of an ancient church. The believers inside were kneeling down. Before each believer was a lamp burning with oil. They appeared to have come prepared to provide their own light. In the front of the church I saw a white lamb.

From out of the church (the isles), flowed rivers of flowers and on the roof of the church, God was pouring out gold dust. Read Isaiah 35 verses 1 and 2.

In this vision of a church, I could see that its ancient atmosphere was indicative of the original church. In the form of a spotless lamb, Jesus visited the church to minster to them from the front; the pulpit and stage area. The believers were very devoted, because their lamps contained oil and were burning. They waited upon the Lord's presence only. The lamb up in front is the one they have come to serve. They are faithful, but few in number. The atmosphere is holy.

The Lord was telling me here that he wants more than those few to be faithful. His heart is big enough for all. He wants to bless us financially (the gold dust), as well as spiritually, so that from out of us, like the original church, shall flow rivers of living water, with a sweet-smelling fragrance (as we see with the flowers flowing from the church). Read Genesis 8 verses 20 to 22; Ephesians 5 verse 2 and Philippians 4 verse 18.

Like the early church members, we should prepare our hearts before going to church, where we worship and offer up our praises to God. Jesus is touched by our devotion. So let us be as devoted as the early church was.

II
Dry land and the promise

In my home church I once had a vision of a great flood of water flowing from the pulpit area. On the surface of the water a vapor was hovering like incense. The word I received in connection with this vision was: "The dry, barren areas are going to bring forth life (fruit)."

Read Isaiah 35; Isaiah 41 verses 17 to 20 and Isaiah 43 verses 19 to 21. These scriptures will uplift you when you are going through a period of spiritual dryness.

On that same day, I saw Jesus riding upon the pale blue waters of the ocean, in a misty haze, which surrounds him. This is the same vapor as that which I saw coming from the pulpit. This incense is blue in color. Read Genesis 8 verse 21; Ephesians 5 verse 2 and Philippians 4 verse 18, for an understanding of the effect of spiritual incense and fragrant offerings.

In this vision we see that Jesus has power over the might of the ocean. He has no fear of it. So with him on our side, we need to have no fears either. A situation may be new to us, but if we ask him to be with us, we will have no reason to fear.

III
Shepherds of the flock

Start by reading Ezekiel 34.

From this scripture we see that it is frustrating for God's flock to turn back towards their required destination, if they have been led astray and have wandered for miles or kilometers. Because then they have to go back over hilltops and rocks which can be barren and dangerous. So the sheep might be hungry, thirsty and tired by then. Some of them may get hurt on the rocks. Others may despair and go their own way, where they might be eaten by the beasts.

The heart of the Lord is after the wellbeing of the flock. His heart bleeds for them. If need be, he will go and look for them himself and woe be to those who chose to neglect them.

Jesus said that he who does wrong and teaches others to do so will be called the least in the kingdom of heaven. Read Matthew 5 verse 19.

Ministers of God go through various experiences together and oftentimes these experiences draw them close to each other. Many times they have a flock which causes them grief. However, they should be careful not to spend a short amount of time and effort on the flock, but more time amongst themselves. Their main aim should be to "feed" the flock. If they fail in this the Lord can take away their position of leadership (Ezekiel 34 verse 10).

In the same verse the Lord says that he will remove the flock from their mouths, so that they will no longer be meat for them—the shepherds. When leaders discuss their flock with a lack of faith (talking about their weak points more than about their good points), they "eat them up with their mouths". According to this scripture we see that this is not a positive situation.

So leaders should be diligent enough to seek out those who stray away (verse 16), those who have been hurt in any way and those who are sick.

In verses 18 and 19 we see that we should remember that the spiritual and scriptural teachings we have received in our early days as born-again Christians, are just as precious to those who receive them now, as they were to us back then. We should not disregard those teachings and blessings, but continue to treasure them in our lives. If it were not for them we would not be where we are now, so we should not ruin the experience for those who come after us.

In verses 23 and 24 we see that, should individual shepherds fail to do their work properly, the Lord will exalt one shepherd who does the work well and he or she will be like a prince or princess to their flock.

This is why we sometimes have a popular pastor with an exceptionally large flock and people say: "He thinks he is something special". This happens when someone truly has a heart for all God's people and does not seek his own gain.

The Lord blesses him and raises him up to the level of a prince.

This shepherd does not scatter the flock. Rather, he gathers them. He does not consider the finances he gets through them, because he knows that he receives from the Lord (verse 27).

Then the Lord will stop the world from speaking evil of that flock. The flock shall also no longer suffer poverty (verses 28 and 29). They will be a famous and prosperous flock according to the world's standards (verse 29). When this happens it is not because they are lost in corruption. It is a sign that God is with them (verses 30 and 31).

Blessed be the name of the Lord!

CHAPTER ELEVEN

I
Jesus' love

The following vision, which I had on 17 November 1998, reminds me of the Sunday school song: "Jesus loves me, this I know".

In the vision I saw myself with the Lord Jesus and he was covered with molten gold, which was dripping from his shoulders, his sleeves and his hands. The gold covered him while he embraced me in his arms.

This was such a great blessing to experience. Clearly the Lord loves us and therefore longs to embrace us. So we should allow him to do this. Here in the vision the gold was dripping like an overflow of anointing. Let us then appreciate his love and anointing which is as precious as gold.

Gold shines and it is lasting. It is beautiful and contains many good qualities, for example: it does not tarnish or rust. So a vision which portrays gold speaks about the precious qualities of a person or an event.

II
Call to ministry

The following day I had this vision concerning the ministry of a certain youth pastor: I saw a young, green leaf at first, then a ripe grape being balanced by the leaf and a branch. Then I saw the stalk on which the branch and leaf were balanced and the whole structure seemed too weak to balance the ripe, full fruit. This strain could cause the branch to break.

The branch clearly needs a smaller fruit which will grow with it to maturity, so that the structure is balanced. Then, at this point of balanced maturity, I see a star (bright as the Morning Star), shine upon the branch, the leaf and the grape.

When I looked again (having the vision continue on a separate occasion), I noticed that the ripe grape which I saw originally was not growing from the branch on which it was "balancing". Instead it had its own branch from which it grew. This branch was behind the original one in the first vision. So the previous vision I had was an illusion, which demonstrated a fact about something which could happen.

I received the following interpretation from the Holy Spirit: The tree; branch; leaf and fruit represent the four seasons of the year. Before bearing its fruit, a tree goes through all the seasons preceding its own season of bearing fruit, which is the fourth season.

In relation to the youth pastor in question, I felt that the Lord was showing me that this pastor had to go through four seasons of bearing fruit. So this would not take a year. It would last four years long and he should dedicate these years towards serving the youth. Four fruit-bearing seasons are equal to four years.

The ripe fruit which I saw was that which we sometimes tell ourselves that we do bear, when it is in fact the mimicking of another, more mature believer's fruit. We would act as if we could prophesy; speak in tongues; see visions; etc.

If we want to carry this fruit the strain of it would break us, because we do not have the specific characteristics necessary to carry it. We cannot pretend forever, though. Therefore we ourselves would break under the pressure, but the stronger believer would remain there with their fruit and also a better view, now that we are out of the way.

I realized that this youth pastor's family might be just a little bit too excited about his growth and promotion. They were very ambitious about his future. So I decided not to speak to him about it, but to pray for him instead, so as not to cause offense. I prayed into his ministry, which then grew amazingly well and on a certain occasion I heard him mention that he had lots still to do in the youth ministry. He was now content in his ministry, which meant that his family was no longer fighting for him to get promotion. He was now so much more excited than ever before; about working with the youth.

Three years have passed since I received the prophesy regarding his ministry. Read James 3 verses 12 to 18. Pay special attention to verses 17 and 18.

CHAPTER TWELVE

Psalm 1

Please read Psalm 1

I had the following vision on 19 November 1998 and it reminded me about the words of Psalm 1; verse 3 in particular.

In the vision I saw a fountain made out of purple tree blossoms. I also saw a girl wearing a floral print dress. Later on the dress changes into a waterfall around the girl and she sings and dances in a huge park. She twirls up into the air as well while she dances.

Round about the park are beautiful, stately buildings. The girl is in total joy and then I see Jesus in the sky, high above her, watching her with a smile, while he holds a bright star in his hand, in front of his face. The light from the star makes his face radiant.

Grey doves from the park fly away, up into the air to some mountains beyond the park. The girl dances with joy until she is exhausted. Then she collapses with contentment onto the grass, with a beautiful bouquet of flowers in her arms. The birds come back down to settle round about her.

At the same time I also had a separate vision of a fountain made out of purple flowers.

To me the girl in this vision symbolizes the church in its righteousness. Here also read Psalm 4, especially verses 6 to 8. We see here a similarity of when the Lord held up a star in front of his face in the vision. The gladness spoken of in verse 7 is that of the girl. In verse 8 we see the same peace with which the girl finally rests. At this point she is safe and in peace.

The purple flowers which form a fountain in the second vision, speak of a royal flow of blessings, which give life in the form of fruitfulness. Life which flows forth powerfully.

This scene takes place in the center of the park and symbolizes life to all who dwell in or visit the park, which is a place of refuge from burdens. Here we find Jesus' love in the form of doves, fruitfulness in the form of flowers, lots of joy and also peace. So we should praise the Lord and then rest in his presence—the park—in order to be refreshed spiritually. The "park" can be any place where you find time to be by yourself and praise God. When you emerge from there you should be totally "recharged", with enough strength and energy to continue with the rest of your day, or night.

The bouquet which the girl holds as she rests, symbolizes to me the gifts earned by her, which come through fruitfulness. The flowers are now no longer just surrounding her, but have been given to her personally. They are organized into a bouquet and this symbolizes order out of chaos. She has earned them through righteous joy and praise. That is why she can rest with peace in her heart. You see, in life we actually make a decision about whether we are going to be joyful or not. We also sometimes make a choice to whine and be miserable.

Also now read Revelation 22 verses 1 to 4. In line with the vision, verse 3 mentions that his servants shall serve him and verse 4 mentions that they shall see his face. So in our trials, we should be happy about the prospect of seeing the face of the Lord one day. His face tells us that all is well.

Part 3
Glory and Purity

Dedicated to all the believers at Hatfield Christian Church, Rhema Bible Church, the Noordwyk Baptist Church and the Kraaifontein Baptist Church, who prayed for me faithfully at the time of my neurosurgery in January 2002.

Thanks and dedication also to Dr Govender and his team, as well as the other staff at Tygerberg hospital, who attended to me during this same period. Last, but not least: to my dear, late mother Elizabeth Lambert, for her endless love and care during my long recovery period. She also prayed on my behalf when I myself was too weak to pray.

CHAPTER THIRTEEN

I
Waiting on God

It is my opinion that waiting does not only occur when we expect a certain event to take place.

Waiting has to be a way of life. It has to do with making choices and reaching out to others, while responding to certain opportunities in life, even though we are waiting for a certain event to take place.

Whenever we do not know what decisions to make concerning certain aspects of our lives, we should wait on the Lord's direction. He will know what to do.

When we do not know whether the time is right to embark upon a certain action we should wait, until we are sure, so that a blessing may follow our actions. Being impulsive can lead us to disaster. We are renewed in our strength then, because we did not wage an untimely battle. The battle should be the Lord's and not ours to fight on our own. The Lord's timing is impeccable. So when we feel rushed and anxious about something, we should know that we are not following His pace. Therefore, things can go wrong.

Read Psalm 52 verse 9; Psalm 104 verse 27; Isaiah 30 verse 18; Jeremiah 14 verse 22; Habakkuk 2 verses 2 and 3; Acts 1 verse 4 and Galatians 5 verses 5 to 6.

II
The Lord in Glory

On 20th November 1998 I saw—in the spirit—the Lord Jesus up amongst the clouds. At first the clouds are misty and hazy. Then they become frosty.

A brilliant, pink light shines from amongst the clouds, behind the Lord. Then from out of the light, a gold ring emerges, with diamonds right around its circumference.

The Lord is balancing a gently fluttering white dove on his left hand. There is a golden light in Jesus' eyes. In his right hand he holds a plant, with the roots and some sand still on it.

The ring here represents the unity of the Father, the Son and the Holy Spirit to me. The diamonds represent the lights in the universe (the stars and planets). At the same time this same ring—if enlarged—also forms a crown, which belongs to Jesus and to those who endure to the end (according to my interpretation). This is a crown of life, which is decorated with diamonds.

The plant which Jesus holds out with a look of excitement in his eyes, appears to be a good plant, but it does not bear fruit yet and is bright green in color.

Here the Lord shows me that he is just as excited by planting (the roots on the plant), as he is about reaping a harvest. So, I would say that planting and sowing of seed should be just as exciting to us. When we have no idea what the outcome of a matter will be, we should still be excited about planting and sowing into people's lives, whether they know the Lord or not.

The fact that this green plant is shown to me at the same time as when Jesus and the Holy Spirit (the dove) are portrayed in glory (the light), shows that planting and sowing are also times of the Lord's glory. They are sacred times.

So we should realize that the beginning stage of any venture in the Lord is a heavenly moment. Its importance should not be underestimated.

Read John 4 verses 36 to 38; Romans 4 verses 16 to 18; I Corinthians 1 verses 26 to 31 (in relation to the plant) and 2 Corinthians 9 verses 6 to 15, with regards to planting and sowing in terms of our finances. Glory is also expressed in the giving of goods and finances. Those you give to will pray for you from their hearts. But even if you think that they will not pray for you, it is important to know that you are being obedient to the Lord.

CHAPTER FOURTEEN

I
Life; goals and achievers

On 20 November 1998 I had the following vision and revelation about the personification of the church in some aspects. The people in the vision each represent a certain section of the church.

In the spirit I saw a row of girls sitting in a waiting room that is L-shaped. Near the door of the room in which the girls sit on wooden benches (which are placed along the wall), is a girl with lively eyes and curly, black hair.

Girl A
This girl has achieved most things in life at a very early age, but she is not very happy with her life.

At a far corner of the room a man is observing all the girls and he is not happy with this girl either. She appears happy on the outside, but there is a mixture of mockery and ridicule in her laughter.

When she appears before the Master he tells her that she should remember her First Love. That would be the only way out of her bitterness and misery. She is not where she should be spiritually, so she needs to change her priorities.

Girl B
Then, there is a girl further down the row, towards the other corner, opposite the man. She is awaiting her turn to appear before the Master, in the same way as the other girls are. She has straight, blonde hair and looks uncertain about her future.

This girl has many talents, but life has been particularly hard on her and in many areas of her life she has begun to lose faith.

When it is her turn to appear before the Master he says, however, that her talents are going to lift her up before God and man. She should not bury them, but be happy to explore and perfect them fearlessly. He tells her that she should hold onto the promises in his Word and that she should abide in his Word as well as in him.

In this vision I feel that God is speaking to certain individuals, while he is also addressing the church body as a whole.

Interpretations
Girl A
To me the first girl represents the original church. That is: the early history of the church where signs and wonders were the order of the day. As the church has progressed and she awaits—sitting on the wooden bench—the second coming of the Lord Jesus, she does not regard signs and wonders as important anymore.

So, because she does not value what God gave in the past anymore, she looks with envy towards the world, which seems to have everything along the lines of providence and joy. This church is set in tradition and expects no surprises. So then, flirting with the world seems to be a harmless distraction. There appears to be more fun out there.

Yet it is not the entire church which feels this way. There are a few who long to go back to the way things were once before, but they keep their sentiments to themselves.

The same also applies to the individual who has seen many miracles and wonders in their church in the past, but because these do not happen anymore, this person is easily distracted by the world. On the inside though, they know that something is missing.

Girl B
The other girl represents the church which knows about everything which God has provided for its spiritual and physical well-being but, because she has often been disregarded and slandered by the ignorant, she has given up the fight and is uncertain as to whether or not she is prepared for the Lord's second coming. So the Master reminds her of his parables. Read Luke 12 verses 34 to 48 and Luke 19 verses 12 to 26. Verse 26 could be confusing. To me it speaks of those who are not blessed of the Lord spiritually, because they do not value spiritual gifts. What they have is only material. This can be lost because there is no eternal value to this kind of possession. It is from the world and not from God.

Faith and hope, however—if exercised—will produce more of their kind. This leads to the evidence of these gifts through more and more signs and wonders in the church.

The world then sees this and realizes that true and lasting provision for one's daily needs and for joy can only be found in the church. The church should be a place where people are taught as well as nurtured, because this cannot be obtained in the world. The world's version is always corrupted.

II
The beautiful cloth

The second time when I saw an enlarged, open vision of the Lord Jesus, he was above the main auditorium of my church. He was in the air above the congregation, with his head way up near the roof and his legs were folded. I grew accustomed to seeing him in that particular setting later on. On this occasion he was wearing his white gown which I feel could be identical to the Church's bridal gown, though I get the feeling that His is more glorious.

The first time I saw him in this place and of this magnitude in church, was when I had my first vision of him. He was about five times larger than life size. On that occasion he just laughed. He laughed for what felt like an hour. I later realized that I had needed deep inner healing back then.

The Lord's gown in this new vision was made up of all kinds of fine, high quality white materials, woven together. There was no point where one could see the seam of where one piece was attached to another. They simply flowed into each other. These materials were: silk; satin; taffeta; various laces;

pearl-embroidered lace; pearl-embroidered satin and other, diamond-studded fabrics. It was the most beautiful thing I had ever seen. No bridal gown on earth could equal it. It flows from the Lord, filling the entire auditorium, going up, around the galleries and further on to the doors.

Two years later I had a vision about parts of this gown with some sprinklings of gold dust on them. This too was glorious. Many miracles took place in our church during these times, for example: people receiving gold dust on their hands during worship.

Interpretation
To me the fact that these different types of white material fit so well together (as if they were knitted together), shows that each material is of a very high quality. That is why they do not wear off from each other and so cause weak points.

This makes me realize that if we as born-again believers are represented by pieces of material, then we should fit into the entire piece of the large fabric. To qualify we should be beautiful and unique, with the strong character of Jesus. If we are not, then we cannot be part of such a beautiful piece of art work. Our edges should be free to overlap onto one another, in order to be finely knitted together. There should be no knots and bits of rubbish around the edges, because they should overlap onto those of another piece and then be knitted into it, in order to form a neat and beautiful union.

Where the edges overlap one should not be able to see where one ends and another begins. This is where we lose ourselves to one another for the sake of love, beauty and unity. In this manner we each let go of our self-centeredness and individual identities. If we cannot live up to these requirements, then surely we cannot be part of this precious garment.

We would then be part of a garment that is not pure white in the first place, because we lack purity and if one piece of fabric is unclean, it defiles the other pieces around it. This garment then would have faded shades of what should be white. It would have blotches and spots. It would also become tattered and torn because of weak points in the fabric—a thing which one would be too ashamed to display. It should be hidden behind a bedroom door and never be worn. If its condition deteriorated further, it would become filthy and it would even be used for dusting and cleaning floors.

At worst I would say that this shameful garment might be given away to someone who is not dear to us—the devil.

Jesus cannot touch the dirty or ugly garment. It can be cleansed by his blood though. Then, through the Holy Spirit, he beautifies it and makes it unique, with a strong texture. However, if this does not happen and the cloth has no purpose and purity in it, the Lord cannot use it and neither can he take pride in it. So we should work on making him happy, or we will be cast out into outer darkness. The Lord will find another garment.

One cannot make silk out of cheap linen. So, if your foundation is self and not Christ, you should know what your end destination would be.

God knows your heart's deepest intentions. So, if you intend to glorify yourself and not God, it is not a problem that developed overnight. It started way back when you thought that your salvation was an effort of your own.

If one piece of material looked glorious on its own, but was lost amongst hundreds of meters of similarly beautiful pieces, the effect of the single, complete and large garment would be stunningly beautiful and breath-taking. So be prepared to be in union with other Christians (in a beautiful spirit), for the sake of Christ.

Please read Malachi 3 verse 17; Mark 2 verse 21; Daniel 11 verses 32 to 35; Revelations 7 verses 13 and 14; John 7 verse 18; Isaiah 28 verses 16 to 29 and Isaiah 6 verse 1.

CHAPTER FIFTEEN

I
The Great white throne

One Sunday (I do not recall exactly when), in my local church, I had a special vision but, in my ignorance did not make much of it. The congregation was singing a song about the Lord sitting on his throne and I had my eyes closed. Then the vision began.

What I saw was a large, heavy, square chair. It was rigid looking and was about two meters high and a meter wide. It was white and gleaming. Upon looking at it more directly, it glittered brilliantly. I realized that it was a throne.

When I looked at this throne more closely I realized that it was completely made up of pearls of all sizes. Then I looked even closer and I saw that in-between the pearls there were pieces of rubies, diamonds, emeralds, sapphire and other precious stones which I do not know. These were studded all over the throne.

I did not understand the vision, because I knew that the Lord's throne was white and yet, here were all these precious stones. I did not realize that in their splendor in the Light, they each reflected a bright, white, light. So the throne appeared to be white. The entire arena in which the throne was situated was filled with a brilliant light.

One day I was going through the Bible and I read a section about the throne of God and its details were described. I was then surprised to note that it was the exact one I had seen in the vision. At this point in my Christian life, I realized that I ought to be more in awe of what God showed me in visions. The visions were not mere films like the ones we watch on screens. They were real and portray the truth; right now and into eternity. They are for a purpose which is much bigger than mere entertainment. This vision represented the truth.

While viewing it from a distance, the throne increased in size and I could see various platform levels on a celestial stage, leading up to the top, where the throne was. It was all so magnificent and marvellous that I could have fainted with awe.

In Revelation 4 verses 2 to 6 one sees that various aspects concerning the throne of God are likened to precious stones. So the color of the throne is not white only. It appears pure white because the precious stones reflect the light in heaven.

Also, thundering and lightning come from the throne in the scripture. This makes me think of a time when I had a divine encounter in my bedroom, on my bed and the holy presence in my room spoke with a voice that was at times like thunder, but I could not make out the words. It was awe-inspiring, frightfully holy and intense with love. So intense that I was sure that I would die that night. He also held me very tightly; as if I was the most precious thing in the world.

The after-effect of such an encounter would leave me riding on waves of love, with that same energy surging through my body, for days afterwards. It happened not long before I had my experience with the brain aneurysm rupture.

II
Feeding the sheep

On 23rd November 1998 I had a vision about the Lord Jesus in a field with a flock of sheep, but the grass of the field has the appearance of water in some places. The sheep were feeding on the grass.

Interpretation
The experience of being out in the field with Jesus and feeding on the word, goes together with being under the influence of the Holy Spirit—if we read the Word with understanding. The word of God is inspired by the Holy Spirit and it speaks about him. So the Word does not exist without the Holy Spirit. The water in the vision represents the Holy Spirit.

Therefore we need the instruction of the Word (feeding), together with the comfort and interpretation of the Holy Spirit (drinking) in our lives, as the sheep in the care of the Lord Jesus, our shepherd.

Sometimes, during deep worship I can feel Jesus' face so close to mine that our faces touch in the spirit and I also look into his eyes, which are full of love for us. He is a loving shepherd.

III
Youth ministry

One of our youth pastors—like anyone else in his kind of position in ministry—just thrives on positive motivation and compliments. So then, the older, more senior pastors should seek to lighten the load of the youth pastors, by making them realize just how important their current ministry is. It is not merely a stage which can be rushed through, or endured with boredom and impatience.

Universally, the youth ministry is very important. The church of God should energize the youth ministry in the same way as the music and film industry does with the youth of the world.

So there is no reason why the youth ministry should be viewed as a mere stepping stone on the way to "real" ministry. Let us take advantage of the youth's sense of fun and adventure, as well as their loads of energy. You never know whether someone will grow to be old, so that you can appreciate them then. So let's give all our dedication to the ministry we have presently been appointed to.

Many temptations occur during the course of a youth ministry and perhaps one does not have all the strength to deal with this on a long-term basis. So then, it is wise for the more mature pastors to work closely with the youth pastors and their wives, to show them that situations do change later and only for the better.

As one grows older it is important to become involved in serving the church as a whole, in order to mature spiritually and to escape the temptations inherent to the youth ministry, e.g. illicit relationships with young girls.

Most importantly I would say then, that a youth pastor should be young, energetic and fun-loving, whilst being committed to a close relationship with God and his own family. He should also consult closely with an older and more experienced pastor. Preferably one with children of about the same age as the youth pastor. The older pastor should be there mainly for moral support. This would eliminate the case of having both pastors experience the same temptations. One of them should be strong, experienced and mature, whilst guiding and interceding for the younger pastor.

CHAPTER SIXTEEN

Earthly blessings from heaven

When a fellow brother and sister in my church were going through a difficult patch, the Lord once blessed me with the following vision to share with them, in connection with their finances: The Lord showed me a field of green corn. Amongst the corn, some pearls lay strewn about. These pearls then connect together and form a necklace, which I then next see hanging around the sister's neck. This same necklace grows much longer and it ends up wrapped around the rest of the family, like an embrace.

In a further part of the vision I saw the sister's kitchen where there were two pots on the stove. They contained red lentil curry and yellow lentil curry respectively.

Outside in the courtyard were large containers, like wine barrels. These barrels contained red wine, as I saw eventually and they were used to fill up a dam in the courtyard.

Then the brother looks surprised, because fine gold dust appears on his wife's hands, suddenly. He takes some of it and rubs it onto her forehead.

Interpretation

Once again, the string of pearls here represents the rewards that come after a series of trials; which have affected the entire household in this instance. The area in which the family has been planting is fertile and is going to produce good, much hoped for results.

The time of harvest has not yet come though, because the fields are still green. The important points to note here is that the ground in which they sowed was fertile and that the seed has been tended well.

It is easy to miss the mark right before harvest time. Instead of drawing strength from the fact that we are in the right place at the right time, we become tired of our circumstances. The people in this vision were rewarded for their hard work done in the past. They were delighted when I told them about the vision I had seen of them.

They were to receive extra glory, because I saw them receiving gold dust from the Lord. This form of blessing and recognition may indicate material gain, or the glory of the Lord upon your life. In either case it is a blessing.

CHAPTER SEVENTEEN

I
A vision of heaven

Heaven is a reality so, when our trials seem never-ending, we can rest in the fact that heaven awaits us at the end of it all. Like pain vanishing from our body after we have taken a good and effective tablet. Like a plate of good food after hours of starvation, it is worth the wait and the suffering. There we will get the beautiful things which have always eluded us in life on earth and we will have earned a reward which nobody can take away or ruin.

I experienced my first vision of heaven in my local center of worship: The Hatfield Christian Church in Pretoria, South Africa. A moving experience, no need to say.

It was on the first anniversary of our late Pastor Ed Roebert's death. He had died on the 5th of July in 1998 during the "March of the Nations" event. It was an international annual march of different churches. We marched through the city center to proclaim the glory of God. Pastor Ed was the main organizer.

His widow, Pal Roebert, was delivering a speech on this day of the anniversary and she mentioned that pastor Ed was happy where he was. From somewhere in my spirit I asked the Lord to reveal this fact to me. What resulted was the first of the most amazing things I had ever seen in the spirit. I called her the following day to share my experience.

In my vision I was immediately caught up into another dimension. The place I saw was engulfed in and somehow reflecting a bright, yet gentle light. The source of the light was not visible. Immediately I saw Pastor Ed. His face was beaming with the delight of a little child. His hand was being held by someone guiding him, but I could only see the hand of this individual.

Pastor Ed was being guided towards a building which looked like a palace. Inside the palace were many glittering objects among which were chandeliers hanging from high, embossed, ivory ceilings. These chandeliers were continuously reflecting lights of various colors.

After this palace he was led by the individual to the next palace and after this to another palace, then another and so it continued. I could perceive in my spirit that he was being presented with these dwellings; he has earned them. Pastor Ed remained excited and delighted by these gifts.

Tears of joy were rolling down my cheeks during this entire experience. The love, beauty and glory of heaven are totally overwhelming.

II
The glory and us on earth

I was filled with the amazing love and warmth which was emanating from the Light, which was present everywhere during the vision I had of heaven (in the above section).

In John 14 verse 2 Jesus mentions that there are many mansions in his father's house and that he is going to prepare a place for us.

So, our earthly yearnings to own large, impressive houses are not sinful, unless we covet someone else's. God wants us to have such things, if we worked to earn them. Jesus walked the earth healing people and feeding the hungry. At the same time he was thinking about the heavenly, beautiful things he knew were in our nature to yearn for.

So do not be ashamed when you sometimes think that you should work on achieving excellent standards of beauty and value for your earthly possessions. Do not worship them though, because they are not alive. God is alive.

A desire for grandeur is a reflection of our Godly nature. That is why we are creative beings; because we form beautiful, great things with the talents which we have received from the Lord. God wanted his own temple to be built according to a standard of excellence. He did not just want any old building. He knows true beauty. We cannot, with our natural minds, imagine the beauty of heaven. It has to be a spiritual experience.

Another vision of heaven I have during worship sometimes, is about the gold paving there, which is actually made up of bricks of gold. This paving covers many streets in heaven and in my spirit I can feel myself walking on them barefoot. During these times I experience a lovely cool feeling in my feet, which is like a balm to me. This lovely feeling goes up, through my entire body.

CHAPTER EIGHTEEN

I
The glory of God in us

We should accept the fact that God is on our side, because we are his children. He is proud of us and therefore we should be proud to be called his children. He wants us to excel in life so that (like any proud father), he can boast of us. He wants us to reflect his glory and shine.

We should always smile wherever we go in public, because we have the answer to life's pressing problems through Jesus Christ. When we smile we draw people towards us and some might then feel free to share about a problem which they might be facing. This way we can impart God's Word and love to them. This is one way of shining for God.

Isaiah 60 verses 1 to 3: Verse 1: "Arise, Jerusalem, and shine like the sun; The glory of the Lord is shining on you!" Verse 2: "Other nations will be covered by darkness, but on you the light of the Lord will shine; The brightness of His presence will be with you." Verse 3: "Nations will be drawn to your light, and kings to the dawning of your new day": Good News Bible.

As the redeemed people of the Lord; born through the blood of his son Jesus into new life and being redeemed from sin by accepting his offer of new life in Jesus, we can see ourselves as the embodiment of the city of Jerusalem here. Read Romans 8 verses 9 to 11 and 16 to 17. Verse 17 b : "for if we share Christ's suffering, we will also share his glory": Good News Bible.

What shines on us on the outside is a reflection of what happened on the inside; causing light to shine through to the outside.

If we accepted the fact that we have a great source of light inside of us in the form of Jesus, we would reflect that light on the outside, by being positive and joyful.

II
Altar call

Why not make a choice today to accept that source of light (Jesus) into your heart and thereafter live with the purpose of reflecting that light daily, whilst studying the Bible to learn more about Him? If you have already done this before, then I know that you do have your inner peace and joy.

III
The purpose of the glory

Naturally we can agree that God would not give us something without a purpose. The glory reflected in the form of light in my vision of heaven, was an emanation of the greatest form of love. This is the love that God gave when he sent his son to live and die on earth; for the redemption of mankind from sin. Read John 12 verses 44 to 50.

Verse 46 shows that Jesus himself is that light. Verse 50 says that the Father's command brings Eternal Life.

Knowing then that we carry this life within us in the form of his son whom we have received, we should realize that we can perform the miracles he performed and love as completely and unselfishly as he did.

In John 16 verses 12 to 15 Jesus tells us that he will send the Holy Spirit to tell us things which he (Jesus) could not tell us when he was on earth. He says that the Holy Spirit will glorify him, Jesus, the son of God.

So then, we will have the purpose of obeying the Holy Spirit and of glorifying Jesus, instead of ourselves. With his glory in us though, we should emanate everything he stands for. We should heal; forgive; teach; feed the poor and comfort the broken-hearted, without taking the credit. We should release them to serve God, not us.

They should love him in us as well as honor him. When we leave them he should remain with them. They do not have to follow and serve us. We experience the joy of living this glorious life when we aim to serve and not to be served. When our intention is to serve, He will provide us with what we need.

CHAPTER NINETEEN

Freedom; humility and reward

In our worship we should be as free as birds and not hold back, so that we can receive our full spiritual blessings. These blessings are far more important and fulfilling than material wealth, because we are changed and strengthened on the inside. This allows us to reach much further than we ever have before in our missions; to make a difference in the lives of others.

When we see God's work in a person after we have ministered to them and prayed for them, we are humbled to think that God has seen our heart's desire for that person and this fills us with joy, which is a wonderful reward, always.

On the 3rd of November 1998 I had the following vision during the morning service in my local church.

1.a. I saw birds circling in the air. This reminded me of us as believers who are free, because we have been delivered from bondage.

1.b. In the second part of the vision the birds come down because someone—whom I can discern to be God—is strewing something on the ground in the way in which one would normally feed birds; by scattering crumbs, or seeds.

2.a. In the second vision I saw Jesus amongst the treetops in the city center of Pretoria. Then I saw a dove coming from his heart and it was covered with gold. The bird flew to the Union Buildings (stately government buildings on a hill in Pretoria), where it shook off the gold in the form of gold dust. Then, when the dove's color returned to white again, it flew back to Jesus' heart and came out with six more doves. All seven doves were covered in gold and they flew to the Union Buildings, where they shook off the gold, all over the buildings in the form of gold dust.

Then each dove returned to Jesus' heart and came out with six more doves and they were all covered in gold, then flew to the Union Buildings where they shook off the gold in the form of gold dust. This process repeats itself many times over: gold covered doves flying in increasing groups of seven.

2.b. In a later vision, I saw grey doves pecking at pearls on the ground with their beaks.

Interpretations
1.a. It takes time for us finally to be free in Christ and we then fly around like birds set free from cages at this point. When we fly we are free. Our problems seem far away and we can focus on bigger, more important issues. We feel powerful and we have a better perspective of things, because we observe them from a detached point of view. Our issues are then not up in our faces.

1.b. At a certain point we have to land though, so that we can feed on our daily bread. We need this to refresh us for renewed strength. Here we take stock of our lives and ask the Lord to guide and to help us.

For those in leadership positions: God raises one up to soar, but one must come down to be blessed. We must become humble again. Read 2 Chronicles 5 verse 7 so that you can be blessed by meditating on the Most Holy Place: His presence.

It is also my personal opinion that every believer is a leader in their immediate community. There is a place where you specifically, should take the lead. Don't wait for someone else to arrive one day.

In Isaiah 31 verse 5 we see that the Lord protects Jerusalem, in the same way as birds which hover overhead, when they are shielding something on the ground. Here in the vision he is also the source of blessings—strewing them around.

2.a. In this vision the Lord is up amongst the treetops, where the birds rest. This is a position for ruling, observation and the assessment of the needs down below.

We see that groups of seven doves flew to the Union Building to shake off gold dust there and that the gold comes from Jesus' heart. So we can say that it is in the heart of the Lord for South Africa to prosper. Also, we see that this should happen in a divine manner, because of the blessed number: seven. The doves are white and they move in groups of seven. So this represents holiness, blessings and divinity. Therefore the government should maintain a state of accountability at the core of their operations, in order for the country to prosper. Righteousness should be the aim of all government dealings. As Christians we should pray for this to happen.

2.b. Next we see that God is blessing some birds with pearls. The pearls form from an oyster in its shell (through a long period of discomfort: refer to chapter 4).

 This happens as the Father prunes us. We should consider being joyful by praising God at such times, because the results are only glorious, beautiful and marvellous! So we should try and praise him through the suffering. The praise lifts our spirits and breaks the bonds of darkness.

Pearls are precious. So we should take care of the Lord's gifts to us and not be like the servant who buried his talent. Read Mark 4 verses 25 to 32 and Matthew 25 verses 14 to 30.

Part 4
Dreams into Reality

The highlights of this part are the dreams I had which were similar to outer-body experiences.

Dedicated to the Bible Study group at the Kraaifontein Baptist Church (under Pastor Don Wilson), which I attended a few weeks after being discharged from hospital in the year 2002.

Thank you Pastor Don for all your assistance: spiritually and materially.

Thanks also to the Felix family: my sister Sandra and her husband Mervin, who also took good care of me at this time.

CHAPTER TWENTY

I
What we eat

Visions of Jesus

During the period of around 24 November 1998, I experienced visions while I had my dinner. Usually when I ate alone.

I would see my plate in front of me filled with pearls instead of my food. This made me realize that food was precious. We do not realize it though, when we have no lack of it, when we are too ill to eat, or when we are in a hurry.

God is the Creator and nobody knows more seriously than him; that we cannot function in our daily work when we do not eat. In 1 Kings 17 verses 1 to 15 we have the wonderful example of how God provided food through the ravens and later through a widow; in order for the prophet Elijah not to starve. This was when Elijah was in seclusion upon the Lord's command. Elijah was contented because he did not suffer from hunger or from thirst. This he could only do by obeying and trusting the Lord's command and promise.

We see how very precious pearls are when we read Matthew 13 verses 45 and 46. Here a single good pearl could be more valuable than all of a merchant's earthly possessions.

So, if we view what we eat in this light, we will truly realize that where there is starvation, people need a portion of food more than they need other worldly goods, however precious those may be. They need the food before we preach the gospel to them.

Also in the dining room during dinner one day, when I was alone yet again, the Lord graced me with his presence by appearing before me in a blue and purple colored gown. These colors portray his royalty and sovereign reign. This kind of event is undoubtedly worth more than to dine in the presence of earthly royalty!

At another time, also in the dining room, I had a vision in which the Lord threw diamonds right around me. I feel that in this gesture the Lord wants us to know that he longs to shower us with his splendor. In John 16 verses 14 and 15 Jesus says that the Holy Spirit will give him glory, because he will take what Jesus says and tell it to us. In verse 15 he says that all that the Father has is his. That includes diamonds, pearls and the gifts of the Holy Spirit. This is all completely glorious and he wants to share all of this with us, so that we are spiritually enriched.

II
New names

When God calls and appoints us to his duty he wants us changed from the old person to the new one completely. When God used Abram and Sarai in the old testament, he changed their names to Abraham and Sarah respectively, because they were to see themselves in a completely new way. This was because he renewed them and wanted to fulfill his promises towards them. They would be fruitful and multiply manifold times on earth: Genesis 17 verses 6 to 16.

Upon his conversion Saul had his name changed by God, because he used to persecute Christians before, but henceforth, he was changed into a Christian himself. So he needed a new identity.

Saul was a Jewish leader, but then he decided to follow Jesus Christ, after viciously persecuting Christians. So he became filled with the Holy Spirit for his task as a servant of God and was no longer called Saul but Paul; an apostle of Jesus Christ. Read Acts 13 verses 1 to 12. God changed Saul's name.

Jacob, Abraham's grandson, was renamed Israel by God because, through him would come all the twelve tribes of Israel, who would be called the Jews. He was renamed Israel because, he wrestled with God and he wrestled with mankind and overcame. Read Genesis 32 verses 22 to 32.

If in the world (in our state of sin), we have become known by certain nicknames, it is my feeling that when we receive the Lord we should alter our entire identity. Firstly; by not visiting the places we frequented before and by not keeping the company we kept while we were in sin. We should also alter our manner of being called, by reverting to our real names. This is even more important if our nicknames have sinful or negative meanings. Read Romans 16 verses 17 to 20 and read Isaiah 62, where God speaks to Jerusalem, the city. This is also the manner in which he speaks to us, his children.

CHAPTER TWENTY ONE

I
Alone

Being "alone in the world" is simply a state of mind. There are too many people out there who do care, but because our focus is on a specific group of people who seem to be cold towards us, we feel alone. Even strangers can become loyal friends, if we give them a chance in our lives. If we are aware of all the potential love out there, we will not feel alone in any challenge we might be facing.

There are so many prospects of friendship out there, therefore we should keep our eyes open; so that we can spot our potential blessings. Just walking with a smile on your face can cause someone to be drawn towards you and wish to know you better.

I had a vision once about a green waterfall going down into a valley, where it forms a stream. This stream becomes a little river of the same green color.

This makes me think of a lonely little believer, up amongst the hills, traveling to the valley down below, in order to wallow in despair. Down there it is difficult to believe that they have ever reached the heights of the hills. Yet all is not lost, because by Grace they will grow and so they will go up a hill again and reach the top. In the meantime, the valley is also a place of beauty and should be appreciated. Here we take stock of our lives and grow closer to God by resting in his arms

The waterfall feels that its natural color—green—is unattractive and murky-looking. It is not clear and blue in color. People do not come from far and wide to see it. This is also how the lonely believer feels: unattractive, unwanted and boring.

What this believer does not remember is that; in order to reach lows, they must be approaching from a higher point, which is indeed often up amongst the hills. They did have an opportunity of being high up, where full joy resides and they will surely return there, if they meditate on the source of the joy.

Another point which the lonely fountain does not observe here, is the fact that it appears green, because of the color of the plants around it .

These beautiful, lush, green plants are growing all around the little fountain, following it down as it becomes a stream and then turns into a little river. It is not so lonely after all. Merely because there are no other streams, fountains and rivers around, does it now mean that it is alone in the world. The plants do not seem important because they are fragile and do not last for long. Yet they are company and their presence and beauty is reflected in the little fountain.

If the lonely believer knew this, they would become very happy little fountains. Then they would see that God has provided for them in every phase of their lives. They might have been very big, brilliant fountains at other stages of their lives, but that does not mean that they are not important to God anymore, or that he has forgotten about them. Neither does it imply that he is no longer providing them with company.

Our present company might seem humble and insignificant. Maybe they are little children or old people and we cannot relate to them. However, they are the only people around us and they are important. They are there for a purpose, because they were placed there for us. They will help to cultivate us, shape us and let us grow as individuals.

They help us grow in love; charity and hope. We would be happy and grow in our faith, if we realized that those humble, good people were placed there by God himself for our pleasure as well as his. Please read Jeremiah 17 verses 5 to 10.

II
Storms in a fountain

On the same occasion as the above-mentioned one, the Lord showed me a fountain inside of which a storm was brewing. This storm can reach its peak and as a result will spray water outwards onto the surrounding rocks.

If this fountain is small and leads into a small dam, which spouts out and trickles as a stream further down the mountain and into a river at the bottom, it would be difficult to reach its destination, because it is very small. It would be hard for it to accomplish its purpose, especially if little internal storms interrupted its flow on its journey down the mountain. The water would form sprays which would splash onto the rocks and partially dry out in the sun. In this way only a tiny portion of the fountain would eventually reach the river. It would have lost its course and its purpose.

In a spiritual sense; anger which comes from frustration on the inside—like the storm inside the fountain—will eventually spill out in all directions, attaining no good purpose. The result of this is that our anger may lead us to hopelessness, because our frustration spills out onto others and they might begin to avoid us. In this way we do not direct our despair in prayer toward God and leave it there for him to direct towards a positive outcome.

An outburst of anger leaves us without a positive end in sight and at the same time this causes more trouble for us than what we had experienced initially. The repercussions of our outburst would not be something we had planned for. The people we hurt thus will no doubt want to let us know how they feel as a consequence and we might not be ready to deal with their reactions.

So let us focus on building bridges and not on harming our relationships. We need to practice self-control and this comes from the Holy Spirit. It is therefore important to think rationally before we act in anger. We should also always consider the fact that; thinking before we speak, is more important than the message we feel compelled to pass on.

When we do not see an outcome for a challenge we might be struggling with, it is not wise to become frustrated and act in anger, because then we will ruin our project instead of building it up. God will work it out in his perfect time, if we give it to him instead. He knows best and we should trust him to do his best for us.

III
Coldness

On 1st December 1998, in a vision, the Lord showed me a waterfall; frozen completely. Also, many small, white doves were flying around this frozen place. There is a wintry scene from here until way beyond the waterfall. On the opposite side of the waterfall is a grey, high rock on which an eagle is sitting. The eagle has golden eyes. It is watching the area below.

Interpretation
A waterfall constitutes a large, spread out area from which water tumbles. If this waterfall represents local Church fellowships then we have the one scenario that, during an icy cold winter season the fellowship, which was vibrant in the summer—like the water in the waterfall—also freezes. Fewer people come to Church.

In another spiritual sense this would indicate a time in our churches, or various prayer groups, when we experience a coldness in our relationship towards one another. During such times our productivity would be at a low level as well, because the coldness or indifference spreads from one believer to the next, so that cooperation is minimal. As a result, certain ministry projects get jeopardized.

The doves here would represent the presence of the Holy Spirit. As the Comforter, he would be there to encourage us to become sensitive to one another's needs.

The surrounding wintry scene would represent the coldness of the world out there. Instead of also becoming cold when the world is full of hatred and malice, we as Christians should offer warmth to thaw the surrounding area. So then love flows, giving life to everything around.

The eagle with the sharp eyes represents God the Father, high up above everything, watching us with all-seeing eyes and not missing a single detail or action. The rock on which the eagle sits is grey and not white with snow. He is not surrounded by coldness and he is far from indifferent, because he does not look the other way. Read Jeremiah 49 verses 16 to 22; Isaiah 59 verses 1 to 4; Isaiah 59 verses 15 to 21 and 1 Timothy 6 verses 10 to 21.

CHAPTER TWENTY TWO

I
Being touched

When we are not accustomed to the move of the Holy Spirit and to the way he touches us, we may be fearful and try very hard not to yield and give over to any kind of manifestation.

On the 6th of December 1998 I was in church for the morning service and the Lord showed me the following scene in a vision: There were clouds of vapour among the chairs on the floor level in the church. Then I saw water in the same places. Some people in the congregation let the water touch them. Others were afraid to let the water touch their feet. They lifted their feet onto the chair seats.

This must not be so, because they view the water in the same light as they would perceive venomous snakes. The desired reaction should be for them to anticipate the moment when the water reaches beyond the level of their chair seats, so that they could soak their feet and their legs.

Please refer to the section called: "The river in the book of Ezekiel", in Chapter 5 of this book.

II
Christmas gifts

On that same day, in accordance with the festive season at hand, I saw Jesus as a spiritual Father Christmas. He was dressed not in red and white, but entirely in gold, with many gifts hidden underneath the folds of his robe.

For the less fortunate amongst us the idea of receiving Christmas gifts is something we do not consider as a right, but as a privilege. Others may never know such luxury, yet God is there throughout all eternity, busy distributing the gifts which we take for granted. Gifts such as the beauty of nature, fresh air, love and the greatest gifts of all to mankind: his son Jesus and the Holy Spirit.

If your suffering is so great that you cannot appreciate the beauty of nature, remember that the free gift of his Son is there to bring us eternal joy and peace. Herein we also find everlasting love and hope for the future. The Holy Spirit is there for us as our only true friend, especially when people let us down. He is all the help we need for whatever our needs may be, because Jesus reaches us through Him.

III
Pearls of love

On the 7th December 1998, I had a vision in which I saw a baby floating on the water of a river. Deep in the pool of water were oysters inside their shells. Inside the shells there were also pearls. Then from the shells the pearls grow into a long string of pearls, which emerges from the water, moving out onto the land and it becomes a chain which goes into barren land areas, wrapping itself around rocks.

To me the baby on the water represents the picture of pure Grace. Apparently nobody is taking care of it and yet it is not drowning or in any distress. We may at times feel completely abandoned. Yet God in all his power, is there to take the best care of us, in the same way as he did with baby Moses, who was drifting on the water in a basket. Exodus 2 verses 1 to 10.

Inside the water on which we drift are all the precious gifts we dream about and pray for, as we see with the pearls in the vision.

The water on top is quiet and peaceful, yet underneath there is serious, but patient activity in the form of the production of precious pearls. This labor in the form of endurance, reaches out to embrace areas of life which have not been touched in a long time. The act of patience grows to form a strong, precious and long chain.

Here we can see that, while we learn to rest in God's peace we will, through patience, acquire the strength of purpose and character to embrace others with these qualities of ours, so that they, in turn, also feel valued and loved (like the rocks).

In order to find rest in the Lord, read what Jesus said in Matthew 11 verses 25 to 30. For endurance read 2 Corinthians 4 verses 16 to 18.

CHAPTER TWENTY THREE

I
His majesty and us

On the 16th December 1998 I had a majestic vision of the Lord Jesus in heaven and he was wearing garments of red; maroon; orange and purple colors. The colors were mingled together. All this is indescribable in beauty and splendor. The robes he wears are very long, with long trains. When I look into Jesus' eyes they are filled with light, love and excitement.

The colors of these robes represent heavenly royalty. If in the midst of our earthly trials, we have only a glimpse of all that awaits us in heaven, it would stop us all from wallowing in self-pity. We are truly privileged, because we are God-loving people, who are greatly valued by him. We know that he has good purposes for our lives. Read Jeremiah 29 verses 11 to 13.

II
Promise of redemption

Around this same period of time, I had a dream about myself and an unbeliever whom I have known for a long time. Although we are currently both grown up, in this dream I am an adult and he is a baby. In the dream we are playing in the snow and we are completely surrounded by snow everywhere. There are also handmade creations of snow in great variety: snow men; snow walls; snow balls; etc.

In the snow the two of us do various fun and exciting things, like making snow animals and throwing snowballs, etc. We are very happy in this dream. The entire area in which we live is covered by snow; everything is white. This is like a snow version of heaven. It is not cold, though.

This simple and very clear dream was a motivating force for me; to continue believing in the possibility that this particular person would receive salvation in his life. At that time he was leading a really lost life, caught up in drug addiction. Today a few years later, he is born-again, washed white, like the snow.

In the dream I am an adult, because I have been growing in the Lord for a long time, whereas he is a baby Christian. We are both enjoying salvation in that our sins are washed away and our lives are clean and white as snow, because of the blood of Jesus. We maintain a life of repentance from darkness, that is why our surroundings are white. Read Romans 5 verses 15 to 19.

III
Holy of Holies

A week prior to the previous dream, I had a very significant dream concerning holiness and the love of worship.

In this dream I was with two female companions, who shall remain anonymous, because I have not shared the dream with them. I do pray for them with concern though. Let me call them Suzie and Lorna respectively.

In the dream the three of us were on a very high mountain peak. Suzie and I could see very far and wide. Even to the very ends of the earth. We could see anything we wanted to and this was awesome.

At some point we go around the bend of another mountain peak and find a cave cleft into the mountain. This peak is shrouded in a holy atmosphere (a highly anointed place), but the cave area inside is the holiest place on earth.

Inside the cave is the cross on which Jesus died, standing there with an engraving of Jesus on it. Then I become distinctly aware of Jesus himself standing next to me. I become aware of the fact that he is talking to me, but I do not have the courage to turn and look at him. The atmosphere is too holy.

At this intense point I have an overwhelming sense of urgency for Suzie to join me there, but I can hear her calling back to Lorna and she does not wish to follow me any further. She does not know about the cave. Lorna on the other end, does not appear to be aware of either one of us anymore. Then I am filled with a sense of deep compassion for her, because of what she is missing and how she would feel if she knew it. This holy atmosphere is intensely beautiful.

The Lord then answers my thoughts by saying: "She cannot come, because she does not love me". He says this with an air of great pity and resignation. Here the dream ends.

In this dream one senses that our ultimate aim in life, whether we know it or not, is to be enveloped in the love, the all-encompassing peace and the intensity of joy which we only find in the presence of God. We need to have regular periods of being enveloped in the power of the anointing.

We should not be looking back and hovering at the edge like Suzie and we should pray for those like Lorna, who do not know what they are missing. They have long ago stopped listening to us preach to them. We should enter into the place of his presence. This can be a quiet corner where you would say a quick prayer, or your time in the bathroom, where you can sing praises to God and thank him for anything which comes to mind. Read Matthew 28 verses 1 to 20.

CHAPTER TWENTY FOUR

Cleansing and Perseverance

As Christians we should keep a clean slate before God and not expect him to humor us when we go wrong. We should also not become complacent and then rest in the little that we do know, just because we hate change, or because we are content to live only with what we already know. In order to reach our destiny in Christ we have to move forward.

On the 15th of December 1998 I had a very interesting dream about myself and my family.

I dreamt that my mother, one of my brothers, a niece of mine and I were on our way to a certain building. We arrived there and in front of the building there were two separate staircases, leading to two separate doors. I went to the one on the right hand side with my little niece. My mother and brother chose the one on the left. This one had a slanting step at the bottom with a sieve in front of it. This sieve had a sink below it.

This makes me think that the dirt from people's shoes are meant to fall through the sieve and into a sink. The other staircase has only steps. I think that this would perhaps be intended for barefooted people. People might perhaps have to remove their shoes, because they were entering a holy place.

My mother and my brother reach the steps on their side but, before they can ascend, they are addressed by someone from the inside of the building, who tells them that it is closed and so they cannot enter it on that particular day. This seems to me to be somebody who is denying them the opportunity of reaching their desired goal; by delaying them.

When I go up the steps on the other side with my niece, a man comes down to meet me and calls me into the building, which at this point looks like a very big house (a mansion). This man looks at us with concern. Once inside, he tells me to rest for a while with my niece, who is one year old.

He then leads us into a simple, but clean bedroom with two single beds, one perpendicular to the other. I become concerned when I see the man himself going to sleep on one of the beds. I am afraid, so I begin to pray in tongues as I lay down on the other bed.

I do not rest for long, before I rise and silently prepare to put my shoes on. I find that my shoes have been lined with plastic while I had briefly slept, so I have to remove the plastic before putting the shoes on again. The noise of the plastic causes the man to awake and so he rises from his bed and silently guides me to a kitchen, where I see chefs busy about their work. I later got the feeling that the man guiding me was a guardian angel.

In the kitchen one of the chefs starts speaking about himself with a tone of self-mockery and it is obvious that he is a homosexual man who is not happy with his life. While he is speaking though, his head falls off and lands onto a serving tray.

Then I become aware of the fact that two other chefs are speaking with self-mockery too. Their lips are moving, but their words are not coming from their own mouths, but from the mouth of the head on the tray. Here I clearly see that the low regard which these people have for themselves, is leading to their destruction for, after a few more moments, the head on the tray becomes silent and then dies.

At this point I leave the kitchen with my niece who—in my point of view—signifies the fact that I should be responsible for new Christians. So should all of us as born-again believers. They have been placed in our care.

We descend the steps but now my brother and my mother are not within sight. Here at the bottom of the staircase, there is suddenly a large pool of dark mud. In the mud there lies a slowly increasing number of human bodies. These are black with mud. Some are still alive and are struggling to survive and save themselves from drowning, but eventually they just sink back into the mud and die. The mud seems to be meters deep.

Eventually there appears to be thousands of bodies in the mud. I find a bridge at the foot of the staircase and I walk across it, over the people who are now all dead and covered in black mud. To me the bodies in the mud represent all the people in the world who are suffering and dying from depression, loneliness and sin. Some try to help themselves, but they can only be helped by Jesus who works through Christians, his Word and through the Holy Spirit.

At the end of the long bridge there is a stretch of green grass and I start to walk across this very large, open field. Here I meet a young lady who joins my niece and myself. We are also suddenly grouped together with a few other children, who are somehow entrusted into our care.

I take the lead from this point onwards. I ask the young lady to hurry, but she has no real concern about escaping the danger of the mud, which might be following us. She seems nonchalant about dying in that mud. I call her and speak to her sternly, telling her not to let my niece walk on her own (because she is too young), but to pick her up and carry her across the grass quickly. We start to run.

Later I begin to lose hope about reaching the other side of the grass, because there are sniping soldiers around who want to kill us. They are shooting at us.

At some intervals we hide inside the cavities of pole-shaped, cement structures.

Here I see that we can escape sin and despair, but the demons still follow hard after us, so that they can pull us back.

As we run, duck and hide, it suddenly dawns on me that I should apply the blood of Jesus over the three of us, because I have a feeling that this will make us invisible to our enemies.

Towards the middle point of the plain area in which we are running, we find people who are covered with brown mud. They appear indecisive as to what they should do. They want to remain in the middle, between the good, safe area up ahead and the danger behind them. They do not fear the danger and seem unconcerned about their wellbeing.

This reminds me of Christians who are saved, but do not make much of an effort to please God with their faith. They remain tainted by sin (the brown mud). After we pass them I lead on, urgently.

Eventually we reach hills with long, rust-brown colored grass. At first we zigzag up the hills, but then I am led to discover that when we move in a straight line, leaping over the grass and the rocks, we move faster. I feel that, in a spiritual context, the significance here is that we should take leaps of faith, whilst walking on the straight and narrow path. In this way we will be protected on our journey through life.

While we travel in this way the enemy cannot see us and so they do not follow us. They have given up.

When I reach our destination, I immediately notice people there who are free from any mud on their skins. They look relaxed; lying under trees on green grass and they are enjoying the shade. I do not know whether my companions have reached this place with me. This is where the dream ends.

Interpretation
The last group of people are apparently resting from their trouble and hard labor. They too have fled and arrived at their destination safely. In a spiritual context these people have overcome trials and temptations and are now resting in the presence (peace) of the Lord. This must be heaven.

At this point please read Ephesians 6 verses 10 to 24.

The people covered in the black mud are very lost, therefore the color of the mud here is at its darkest (sin and despair). They are close to losing the battle, because they have made the wrong choice in life. The people covered in brown mud still have a chance of survival and that is why the mud here is not so very dark. The people at the end have no mud on themselves at all, because they are completely out of danger. They have conquered sin and bondage, through Jesus and with the guidance of the Holy Spirit.

CHAPTER TWENTY FIVE

Fully blessed

We might think that we will never reach the point where we are blessed completely. Yet this place does exist; if we are totally obedient and rest in the Lord completely. So it is up to us after all. We can be totally at peace.

Early in the year 2012 I dreamt that I was working in a very large restaurant but, I am always very late and so I have no clients to serve. My fellow waiters look at me with concern and keep reminding me that, unless I start arriving on time, I will never earn any money. This being due to the fact that we are working for tips only.

So I plan to tell my mother that I will have to find a place amongst the shacks (informal settlement), where I can rent and live, because the restaurant is close to the vicinity of the shacks.

Then I become worried, because I also want a big, beautiful house in the suburbs, like the area in which my mother lives. I need a different kind of job in order to have this though. I realize however, that the food I get at this restaurant for my waiters' lunch, is so delicious and great in variety that I don't want to leave it. This causes me to choose to continue working there, even without a salary. I get pure butter for my bread. I also get eggs; bacon; chicken strips; etc. These are all prepared for me by the chefs. The other waiters tell me that I should not be eating, because I do not arrive at work on time. This does not cause me concern though and I simply continue to enjoy my food.

I discover later on, that there is another kitchen at the further, opposite end of the restaurant. When I arrive there, I find a counter on which cocktail sausages in a delicious-looking red sauce, are arranged on a plate. There is also some seafood on a side plate. This is very tempting to me and so I start eating it all. One of the chefs there asks me whether I am enjoying the sausages and whether they are mine. I reply with uncertainty in my voice and agree that they are mine.

Later on I see a cousin of mine who has passed away a few years ago and he asks if I have tasted "this new kind of tuna fish". The fish he shows me is large and looks like red jelly with small, black seeds in it. I taste it and it has a deliciously fragrant, sweet-sour taste. So I have really large helpings of it.

When I get home later I tell my mother about this delicious new tuna fish and she looks at me incredulously. So I assure her that the black seeds are like the black spots on the outside of a strawberry. I tell her that they are not black because of evil.

Interpretation

The fact that I am constantly being reminded about the fact that punctuality is important, shows that the other waiters are concerned about me. This wonderful place with its amazing food, represents heaven and in order to enjoy heaven's benefits, I should know that time is running out for everything I have to do here on earth. I have to work hard to be on schedule. Time is an all-important factor.

To understand the importance of punctuality read about the five wise virgins and the five foolish virgins in Matthew 25 verses 1 to 13. Here we see how sweet sleep can be but, if we know that we might need sleep or anything else that may come in the way of us not reaching our goal, we should make preparations for such situations in advance. Therefore we cannot postpone our obedience to the Lord, because we do not know the day when he returns, or the time when we depart from this world on our dying day. So we should remain alert.

The concern which the other waiters in the dream have for me, is similar to when in life, we find that family and friends look at us with concern and constantly remind us that we should get our act together. This happens when they notice that we have a slack approach to life. In another sense we may find that—if we are unsaved and lost in our sins in very obvious ways—Christians will tell us to make our lives right with God.

In connection with our calling, we might be busy putting off the launch of the ministry which we know we are called to. So people around us at church will keep on reminding us about this fact. What is important to note here is that those people will not always be there, acting as our conscience.

Eventually they will stop reminding us about our duties towards our ministry in the Lord.

It is clear here, that I really want to have this job in my dream. However, in order to work in this place with its wonderful food, I have to humble myself to the point where I would have to live amongst the shacks. The degree to which I love all this special, decadent food shows that I really do value good things, as we all do. The restaurant is a stark contrast to the area of shacks not far behind it. This shows that one can find something very valuable in a really humble place. If we are humble, we go to heaven one day and we also already do have heaven inside of us.

The special tuna which is like red jelly and which tastes so exotic and decadent, makes me think of the blood of Jesus, in the spiritual sense. The sanctification and the power of the blood of Jesus is invigorating and pleasant to us when we apply it over our lives spiritually.

The fact that my late cousin shows me how wonderful this red fish is, might imply that, at the time of his death, he did accept the sacrifice of the blood of Jesus for his life, even while he was being murdered. He clearly wants me to know this and perhaps to tell it to others, because the red stands for the Blood and the fish stands for souls which must be saved. The red fish represents the saved soul who is sheltered by the Blood.

The fact that there are two kitchens at opposite ends of this restaurant is unusual and very significant. If this restaurant represents heaven though, it is only natural that a double portion of provision is supplied. Even while on earth, God can give us double and overflowing portions of blessings, like when David says that the Lord makes his cup run over, as God anoints his head with oil in Psalm 23 verse 5. Also, in 2 Kings 2 verse 9 Elisha asked for a double portion of Elijah's spirit. He did get this and as a result he could do twice as much as Elijah did. Also read verse 14.

May God bless you as you follow in his footsteps. He will always provide the strength for you to overcome your earthly obstacles as in 2 Kings 2 verse 14, when he showed Elisha his power.

CHAPTER TWENTY SIX

I
The impact of war

During a certain period of the year 2010, I began to have a series of dreams about me being in Iraq and in the dreams I was an Arab. I was often running, ducking from bullets and hiding from American soldiers. I was seriously filled with fear for my life.

At certain points I found myself standing in a line-up with other Iraqi soldiers, waiting to be executed by gunfire. My turn would arrive and in some dreams I escaped, but in others I perished. At that point I would wake up from the nightmare.

During those times I felt that the world should realize sometimes, that Iraqi people also walk around with fear of the worst to come at any given moment.

The fear which I experienced in these dreams was so very real, because God wanted me to know that he loves these people too. The women and children suffered fear and anxiety without being responsible for all the trauma. The soldiers don't have a choice.

In its entirety, I feel that war is ugly beyond anything else on earth.

Sometimes we are at war with ourselves, with the mind being the battlefield, so we sabotage our own projects in life and thereby our progress. Here we need to block out the ugliness with the Word of God.

Some religions or cultures teach that, if we are really beaten down by failure, we can restore our honor by committing suicide. The Bible however, does not recommend this. Your potential is a powerful weapon and people need to see it.

II
Gifts

On the 5th of November 1998 I had the following vision: I saw a great, golden fish eagle rising up from the ocean and it flies out to the city, where drops of water from its wings drop down onto the inhabitants of the city, but before they land, they are turned into pearls.

The drops of water are from the ocean, so they are salty, like tears. Pearls also come from the sea, unless they are fresh water pearls. In this instance they are from the sea. A pearl forms slowly, with patience and long-suffering.

Revelation
In this instance I feel it is safe to say that the eagle represents the Holy Spirit. Also, I want to say that pearls are good, pure, perfect and precious. God wants to give us good, beautiful and perfect gifts, if we hold on and don't give up. God is mighty, like the eagle.

So then, we must first realize that when we suffer for a cause in Christ over a long period of time, it is because something perfect and good will result in the situation. Please read Ezekiel 17.

III
Victory over a demon

On the night of the 6th November 1998 I had a difficult experience as I tried to sleep. For a couple of weeks before this, I had experienced visitations from a female demon, who used to call me from the passage, around the door of my bedroom. I could hear the voice, but I could not see the one who was calling. She hid herself.

When I ignored her—because of something my father had once said to me about not answering when one does not know the identity of the one calling—I sensed that she grew very angry. She would then turn away and leave.

On the night of 6 November 1998, I sensed something in my room and I woke up, carefully opening my eyes and I looked to where I sensed the presence. I saw an extraordinarily tall, slim female dressed as an alien with antennae attached to her head. Her face was covered by a mask.

I knew immediately that this was no Alien. It was an evil presence and I also sensed that this was the owner of the voice which called to me so persistently. She moved stealthily towards my wardrobe and was just about to open the wardrobe door, when I rebuked her and she left my room in haste.

On this particular occasion she returned to my room later and I was asleep, yet again. She was immediately upon me as I awoke. She had a mask on and through my spirit I told her that I would remove the mask and expose her face. I did this very quickly, using my physical hands.

The face revealed to me was ugly and from it I sensed an intense spirit of hatred mingled with envy. In the middle of the face was one eye, situated on the forehead. It was the only eye she had. There was no nose and a completely round mouth was just below the eye, from which the hatred burned.

Then she said something which chilled me to the bone: "Now I'm going to turn your light out." Usually I sleep with my door open and with the passage light on. So actually there was light but, immediately after the demon said this, she flicked off an invisible light switch to the left of my bed, near the window. My actual light switch is about three meters away, near my door. Almost instantly, I was plunged into a darkness such as I had never experienced before. It was completely cold and dark with evil.

Then she started to choke me, but from inside of me something lurched out. My physical body otherwise was totally petrified. This other body came out of me and for what felt like about three hours, I wrestled with this demon. I then clawed at her and felt her flesh turn to minced meat under my nails. I completely squashed her to a pulp, then I fell into a natural sleep.

From that night onwards, the demon never returned to call me, or to stand around in my room and it did not return to attack me either. I feel that the Grace of God was with me in helping me overcome this terrible challenge.

The above visitations started one night after a new lady in our church cell group gave me a lift home. I did sense that something about her was strange. She was an airhostess and began to visit at our cell group worship once, every couple of weeks, when she was in our city.

She never said much and always seemed a little mysterious. She did not pray when it was her turn to pray, but we did not put any pressure on her. One evening she finally confided that she had nightly visitations and that she experienced strange and disturbing phenomena, whenever she went to bed. This happened, regardless of which city of the world she found herself in. After she shared with us we prayed for her and the visitations stopped in her life.

These kind of phenomena often occur when one has opened a door to them by attending occult ceremonies, watching such movies constantly, or after persistently reading such material.

CHAPTER TWENTY SEVEN

I
Protection of an angel

The next extraordinary experience in my bedroom occurred one morning, before I woke up, at around 6 o'clock in the morning. I sensed a presence in my bedroom, but because I was physically so tired and so accustomed to demons in my room during that period of my life, I did not bother to open my eyes. I merely said: "Go out in Jesus' name".

I sensed that nothing had happened, so I repeated my command, but again I sensed that the presence had not left my room. I repeated the command for the third time and still nothing happened, so I opened my eyes. Immediately I sensed that I should not look directly at this being, so I looked into the television screen at the foot of my bed to see its reflection, because the television set was off.

On the screen I saw a small lady dressed in white, with a cross in front of her chest. The cross was also white. Her hair was short and golden in color. She appeared to be watching me with a surprised look on her face. She seemed to be surprised about the fact that I was rebuking her and yet she seemed peaceful. I became aware of the fact that she also appeared to be listening to another voice.

She observed me silently and with interest for a couple of minutes and then did something strange. She turned around in an unusual manner. Her front simply changed and became her back, but the cross remained in place. So now I could see her back, with the cross on it. A few seconds later she simply vanished. I experienced a wonderful feeling of peace as I went back to sleep.

I don't know why this angel visited me. All I could think of at the time, was that she came to protect me from something and that she would not leave until the danger was gone. She would not listen to my orders, because I was not aware of what was really going on. All I wanted was to return to sleep, because I usually went to bed late and as a consequence, I would be very tired around that time of the morning. Read Psalm 91 verses 1 to 6.

I thank God for his protection and his sovereign power.

II
The anointing and the anointed

Within a couple of weeks after I had the vision of the dragon being slain by the power in the blood of Jesus, I had another vision about it. I saw the dragon behind a mountain. This time it seemed much bigger. From a cave inside the front of the mountain, water was gushing out.

At the back of the mountain, behind the dragon, a great current of water (as powerful as the ocean), was coming in towards the mountain and towards the dragon. The dragon appeared afraid of possibly drowning in the flood which was coming up. It seemed really anxious.

What the dragon did not know, was that there was another surge of water coming from the front of the mountain as well. Apparently the cave is the home of the dragon, but now the cave was no longer inhabitable. It is clear that the dragon would be defeated by water this time, because it could not escape either to the front or to the back.

The fact that the beast can always be defeated, no matter how big it becomes, is because of the faith and the prayers of believers. Those Christians who hold onto the power that exists in confessing Jesus as Lord. He is the one who died and rose again. The one whose blood defeats all evil in order to protect the righteous.

Read 1 Chronicles 16 verses 19 to 25. In verse 22 the Lord says: "Do not touch my anointed ones; do my prophets no harm." Here in this scripture he clearly shows his attitude of protection towards his people.

The power of the beast therefore exists only by appearance. It has no true power, because it has no Real source. To be defeated though, the dragon needs to be reminded of where its limits are and this should be done by the authority of the name of Jesus. It cannot rule over God's anointed ones. Therefore we can say that the state of being anointed is protection in itself, because then we speak and move with authority.

The power of the anointing also comes in the form of water (the river of life in Ezekiel). So the water here in the vision represents the anointing which overcomes the evil.

Therefore as ministers, our anointing should always overcome the evil attacks upon our lives, because we hear the voice of the Lord clearly.

III
Unity

I had the following vision during a morning service at my church (the vision originated a few weeks earlier, at a prayer meeting, while we were worshiping): I saw several pastel colored scarves in the Lord's hand. I interpreted these as representing the individual gifts of the prayer group members, respectively. Then the Lord took them all and pulled them through a golden wedding band. I feel that the wedding band represents the unity of the Father, Son and the Holy Spirit. This unity—as the ring—also has no beginning and no end.

The scarves come out at the other end of the ring in the form of a single, beautiful, multi-colored scarf. I saw here that through the Father, the Son and the Holy Spirit, our gifts in the prayer meeting should function as one. So nobody should hold back their particular gift.

We sometimes feel happy to watch someone else's gift in action. Most of the time we feel that our own gift is inferior. We might feel too shy or terrified to even utter a word, let alone bless the meeting with a word of revelation, encouragement, knowledge or wisdom.

However, true glory to God is achieved when we are obedient to the Holy Spirit; who will guide us as we speak or offer assistance. In this way we may bless people in ways they would never have expected. Holding back can then be considered to be: the withholding of a blessing which might have been very important to some specific person. Read 1 Corinthians 12 verses 28 to 31 and 1 Corinthians 13 verses 1 to 7.

A few weeks later in church I saw the Lord pointing out this multi-colored scarf to certain areas in the church. I sensed that he was pointing out the amount of unity we had in church at that time. It showed that only about 7% to 10% of the ministries in the church were functioning in proper unity. I feel that the church would flourish as the Bride of Christ if all ministries made time and allowances for one another. Each ministry is vital and should be recognized and encouraged by all the others. Pride should be avoided at all costs.

Part 5
Future signs

Dedicated to Chantelle. May the Holy Spirit always guide and comfort you.

CHAPTER TWENTY EIGHT

I
Who's will?

In our relationship with God we go through stages when we struggle to pray and to study his word. This is natural in any relationship, because we also go through periods when we struggle to communicate with friends or family.

However, there are times when a person who has just read the word of God—or spent time in prayer—can be aggressive, difficult to please, irritable; etc.

What brings about such an uncharacteristic result after "spending time with God"? Was the purpose for this devotional period one which was motivated by their church, whereas this particular believer has perhaps not made it their own priority?

The purpose of daily devotions is for us to develop a closer relationship with God, to set the day off on a good footing in the morning and to thank him for his faithfulness at the end of the day. We continue by asking protection for the night ahead. Together with this, we should also read through his word, as we seek his face.

If we miss out on the true purpose of this moment we will feel disillusioned, instead of encouraged by this time which we supposedly enjoy with the Lord.

I feel that there should be a separate time of the day for us to lay our trials and problems before God. Then we do not attempt to put too much into this limited time in the mornings, when we are rushed or at night when we are tired.

If we find the time we can then reflect on what we have asked him. We can consider whether we have asked according to his will or ours. We can then also appreciate the fact that our timing for an answer should be in line with his, so that we don't lose our hope.

If, however we have never yielded ourselves to him, we will have no desire to know or seek his will in the first place. We will seek our own will and will even find ways to help ourselves, in order to have our needs met. Our prayers and Bible reading sessions would then only be done with aims to satisfy our selfish wants and desires. In this way we can be disappointed.

So then, if we are unsuccessful in getting what we want, we will be frustrated and angry. We will despair. Please read Romans 12 verses 1 to 3 for guidance in your prayer life.

Prayer should leave us feeling strong and hopeful enough to go on with our lives. Our spiritual energy should be recharged after praying.

II
The gift of marriage

Through the Holy Spirit I received the following words on marriage on 16 December 1998. It was an interpretation to a message which I had received through a Tongue (spiritual language): "As I can reconcile all men unto me so can I reconcile all marriages to me because I am God. I love and I forgive. Nothing is too hard for me. I can do anything. If you abide in me and my words abide in you I will make your marriage a sweet-smelling flavor in Christ Jesus.

Don't ever let anyone make you feel that you are connected to the wrong person, because I give and see potential in all men to do right. Don't put your trust into princes and in men. Put the prospect of your marriage into my hand and I will guide, shape and form it. No man knows the future but I. Do not let any person on earth come against your love, because I gave it to you. It is your precious gift.

Your wedding does not depend on who will and will not attend. It is all about my will. I am the one who is in it and I will be there.

Your marriage in my hand is a jewel; a diamond, but it is also a weapon. It is like a two-edged sword because it is centered around my word. It is a sword in my hand because the two of you shall be one and you are warriors; each one of you in their own right. The two of you are one."

I was very encouraged by this powerful word from the Lord. It applies to many born-again couples out there who are contemplating marriage, as well as to those who are already married.

CHAPTER TWENTY NINE

I
Be encouraged

Around 19 December 1998 I received the following vision with regards to my church congregation: I saw Jesus parting an ocean. At the parting (in the center) there were fishes on dry ground, flopping about and causing dust. The fishes on the right side of the parting—who are still in the water—dive to the center, into the dryness and then spew out coins to the fish which are there. These fish which have been dry for a while now, are growing weak from the lack of water. Soon the coins cover these fishes and the other fishes which brought the coins, dive back into the water.

Afterwards, the water covers the parting and the coins wash out onto the beach, but all the fish remain in the water. The weak fishes have been revived by the coins.

Interpretation
The "river of God" is the flow of the manifesting presence of the Holy Spirit. All rivers run into the ocean and so does this one. In the spiritual ocean there are times when the Lord must make a path, not for anyone to pass through, but for those fishes without guidance to be exposed. Then the

others who follow the guidance of the Lord should strengthen those who are weak, by striving through sacrifice; giving of what is precious to themselves, in order to help the weak and struggling ones.

This means that the strong believers should cover the weaker ones with their spiritual gifts of love, concern and also with prayers where needed. In this way they assist them practically, until God wills to cover their spiritual dryness completely and allow them to be revived.

The stronger believer though, should not be caught stuck in the middle. They should follow divine guidance by listening to the Holy Spirit. They should also obey the written word of God and not be affected by the slack behavior of others.

Isaiah 41 verses 17 to 20 tells of how the Lord views the weak amongst us. Those who are weak in faith will not be forgotten by the Lord. He promises to take great and exceptional steps to re-establish them before him. Then, when they are strong, the Lord says of them in verse 20: "so that people may see and know, may consider and understand, that the hand of the Lord has done this, that the Holy One of Israel has created it."

So, if you are spiritually weak, you have every reason to trust God to strengthen you. On the other hand, if you are strong spiritually, never hesitate to give of your precious time to those who need a word of encouragement and the love which they do not receive at home. Then do not forget to spend time with the Lord, so that you can gain more of his love and wisdom. He will be your source of strength and guidance so that you don't run dry from giving.

II
Relationships in Christ

Through what I believe was a message from the Holy Spirit, I once received the following words on Christian relationships:

1. Spend enough time together. Not too little, so that you have only a vague idea of one another's identities and not too much, because then you lose your sense of individuality and your intimacy with God.

2. Do in-depth Bible study together.

3. Pray together. Make an appointment for prayer and stick to it.

4. Gain interpretations to divine dreams and visions, together.

5. Talk about your lives—past and present. Try hard not to keep secrets from one another. They catch up on you at some point.

6. Share and help with one another's problems and trials.

7. Be each other's helpmeets (soul mates). Where one struggles with an issue, the other should look at it from their point of view and come up with considerate suggestions to help.

8. Take things one day at a time: Do not rush to your destinies (marriage or children). Leave your destinies

to God, who will do things in his time. Do not be motivated by fear or anxiety.

9. Cultivate a relationship with someone who has enough inner strength; a strong sense of individuality; determination and a desire for God's will in their life.

10. Don't leave anything up to chance: if you want something to change or happen in your relationship, pray about it first, then bring it to the table.

III
Moving into the mission field

In my ministry at this stage, I sensed that the Lord was guiding me towards using my talents in such a way, that I could follow my calling. This could be reached by applying my talents to my outreach ministry. My talents should not take precedence, because I know that I was not only called, but was also chosen for my ministry at a young age. My talents developed later, even though they were there at the age of five. I was chosen before then.

This I know because, anything in my life which was not directly stemmed from ministry, was very clearly denied me. When I turned out to the left or to the right I was always pulled back sharply. I have been aware of this for years now. The ballet; music; business and mathematics should not be the main focal points in my life. They are means through which I show others that God is the Creator. They on their own, are not worthy of worship and adoration, even though I have a passion for them.

When I indulge in my favorite activities in life, I should also have God with me and place him at the top of my priorities. These things may impress me a lot, but God should occupy all my plans. When you are handpicked (commissioned) by Jesus he warns: "If you put your hand to the plough and look back, you are not worthy of the kingdom of heaven." This is a very serious statement. Read Luke 9 verses 61 and 62.

Once I have sacrificed something I love for the sake of the ministry, I may not constantly think back about that thing, because then I will not be used by God in the future. Lot's wife was turned into a pillar of salt, because she looked back on the city which she had fled: Genesis 19 verses 15 to 26.

The Lord led me to realize that I should move about with Christians who can share my anointing while I share theirs, because then we will learn from one another. We should be at more or less the same level spiritually, or the mediocre one will cause the strong one to become slack in their commitment or become frustrated. This is simply a fact.

I also sensed then, that God wants me to go to various churches around the world and not stagnate in my spiritual life. I should not remain stuck in one church, growing accustomed to my seat there. Then I will learn about how other nations love the Lord and one another. I will also learn how to be an asset to them.

The following happened on the first day of January 1999: I received a message which was inspired by the Holy Spirit. The message said that I had to lead people to the Lord and encourage them to plant churches. I was also inspired to record what the Holy Spirit teaches through me; either on voice recording instruments; in writing; or on video. All these recordings of outreaches are important; to remind people about the messages that went out on that particular occasion.

Everything I received in my spirit then was later confirmed to me in August of that same year, when I attended the Outreach and Missions course at my church. This course was very blessed. This is where I miraculously received gold fillings in my teeth, during worship. Whilst on this course, I was challenged to write on various subjects.

CHAPTER THIRTY

I
Baptism

Also on the first of January 1999, I received the following vision from the Lord: I saw the Lord Jesus standing by a riverside. There was lush plant growth on both sides of the river. Then again Jesus was in the water and was holding a beautiful lady, by balancing her head between his hands. Her head was above the water and the rest of her body was under the water. She had stars in her eyes, because of her joy. She was obviously also in sweet, spiritual communion with the Lord. Opposite the river, a white dove was perched on the branch of a tree.

The sun was filtering brilliantly through the branches of the tree and it was a glorious sight. Time stood still in this atmosphere of perfect peace; beauty and harmony. This vision was very touching, because of its true and unique beauty. It speaks to me clearly about the wonder of water baptism in Christianity and also about how important this is to the Lord.

Water baptism is not merely a formality for a born again believer. It is also a deeply spiritual experience, whereby the

Holy Spirit is also present (as we see with the presence of the white dove in the vision I had). We see the equivalent of this, when we read about the appearance of a dove and a voice from heaven, when Jesus was baptized by John the Baptist. The dove here also represents the Holy Spirit.

Because this experience represents spiritual rebirth, it is filled with great joy and spiritual rejuvenation, as we see in the vision.

Please read Matthew 3 verses 13 to 17 and Acts 2 verses 32 to 38.

In these scriptures we learn that baptism in water is a prerequisite for enjoying a complete life as a Christian. One should first accept Jesus as one's personal savior, then one should be baptized in water, in the name of the Father, the Son and the Holy Spirit.

Water baptism is symbolic of laying down the old life, to take on the new life as a born again Christian. We go into the water as one person and come out as a new person. The old person has died and a new one emerges from the water.

In the Bible water symbolizes cleansing as well as spiritual life. So, with being immersed in the water, we expect and accept that we are symbolically being cleansed, as well as being given new life—eternal life. By the time we emerge from the water we are completely new.

In Mark 1 verses 4 to 8 we have John the Baptist speaking on baptism and the forgiveness of sins. He shares on the baptism of water, as well as the baptism of the Holy Spirit. From verse 9 to verse 13 we have the baptism of Jesus.

We see the effect of his baptism as he emerges from the water, for immediately as he comes out of the water he sees heaven open up and the Holy Spirit descend upon him. Here we have our first occasion of water baptism, followed by the baptism of the Holy Spirit. Jesus was baptized in preparation for his ministry on earth.

The river Jordan here is the same river in which Naaman had to dip himself seven times, to be healed from leprosy. Read 2 Kings 5 verses 1 to 15.

We see here that Naaman was unclean because of his skin disease. He was contagious. So are we when we are in our sinful state. This however changes when we accept the Lord and are baptized. When we are cleansed from sin we become as innocent as babies. This is the same as when Naaman's skin became like that of a young child, as we see in verse 14. We become new people. Free from the past and free from sin.

II
End Time Signs

On 2nd January 1999 the Lord gave me a vision about the Lord Jesus in a spiritual atmosphere of vapors. These were soft pink mingled with baby blue, in color. (I often also saw these colors in the Spirit whenever I visited at Rhema Bible Church).

These vapors surrounded Jesus. Then I saw him handling pink satin material, as if he were testing the quality and texture of the fabric. Amongst the fabric were large, pastel colored pearls. I feel that these pastel colors represent grace and love, because they are soft and gentle.

After this I had a vision of Jesus sitting high above everything, up in heaven and rather solemnly beating a crystal drum. I sense here that he is doing this in order to symbolize the passing of time, in the same way as the ringing of a church bell indicates the time and calls people to church for specific occasions. So Jesus is telling us that the time for his second coming is approaching. This will be the most spectacular event for the world to experience. He is also telling us to use our time wisely, because it is a precious asset.

The soft colors in the atmosphere surrounding Jesus in the first part of the vision portray gentle love and kindness. Then the material he handles in the second part of the vision speaks of us in his hands. When he works with us we should be as soft and as beautiful as satin. At this point, because of our perseverance and strength in faith, we are also as precious as pearls.

So, we should allow the inspiration of the Holy Spirit to guide us towards being gentle and longsuffering, because only then do we become beautiful in his sight and as valuable as pearls in his hands. Read Isaiah 29 verses 15 to 24; Isaiah 48 verses 1 to 22 and James 5 verses 7 to 20. Study these scriptures and observe, according to your own understanding, how God wants to work with you.

Soon the Lord will return. Read Matthew 24 verses 1 to 51. This is where Jesus describes the terrors which will befall all those who did not prepare for his second coming. He also describes the signs which will precede his second coming.

Isaiah 29 verses 15 to 24 shows us that it is useless for us to think that we can do things without God knowing about them. Such plans will not bear good fruit. If what you have planned is too precious to share with anyone, remember that it can only prosper if you tell God about it and you allow him to guide you in your quest towards achieving what your heart desires. Verses 18 to 21 show how God will eventually bring justice to earth. Verses 22 to 24 show God restoring his people and blessing them with knowledge and with wisdom.

In Isaiah 48 verse 3 the Lord says that he has predicted long ago what would happen and that he made it happen suddenly. So we should not trust in our human understanding of how to interpret and respond to signs of the times, because God can make events to occur suddenly.

In verses 4 and 5 the Lord tells us that he knows how we will act when our nature is stubborn and unyielding. He remains ahead of this kind of response, because he predicts our actions.

In verses 6 to 11 we see that God tests us and that he will not share his glory.

In verse 15 the Lord shows that when he leads us he will give us success in our missions in life.

Verse 17 says that God teaches and directs us for our own good. So then, when things go wrong, we cannot say that God has led us astray. When we follow his commands (verse 18), blessings will flow for us and we will have victory in our situations.

In verse 21 we see that he provides for us in difficult times. They will not defeat us.

James 5 verse 7 teaches us to be patient and to keep our hopes high for the Lord's second coming. When we hope our faith is active. Our actions portray our hope in that we are joyfully expectant. We do not have to be begged to be cheerful. His coming should be our joy and hope from day to day. So we should be patient and stand firm (verse 8).

Verse 11 tells us to be at rest in our trouble, because we know that God is full of mercy and compassion. He sees our tears and brings about the required outcome.

Verse 13 says that when we are in trouble we should pray. Sometimes only God needs to know your trouble. Not everyone needs to know. It says that when we are happy we should sing praises to the Lord. So we do not have to over-indulge in liquor, or wild parties when we celebrate.

Verse 15 shows that with the healing (through the prayer of faith and the anointing with olive oil), comes forgiveness of sins.

Verses 16 to 18 show how earnest prayer and righteousness is very powerful.

Verse 19 tells us not to ignore the believer who strays away (when they return to the world). We should bring him or her back, so that they do not perish in sin.

In the first few verses of Matthew 24 Jesus tells that war; famine and earthquakes will be the first signs of the end. He says that earthquakes will be in various places.

Then follows the persecution of Christians. Those who endure and do not give up their faith will be saved. By this time the Gospel will be preached everywhere, to all mankind. Then the end will come.

The end will come when the "terrible terror" comes in the holy place: verses 15 to 22. This speaks of terrible things like war and fighting in Jerusalem, which is the "holy place". At present both Jews and Muslims (as the descendants of Abraham, through his sons Isaac and Ishmael respectively), want to have possession of Palestine.

This will also be a time for false prophets and false Messiahs performing false miracles, to deceive even the very elect: verses 24 to 25. So watch out.

Verses 34 to 44 show that though we marry and continue with our lives we should expect his return. Temporary issues of life should not be our main focus.

The activities of earning a living; buying vehicles and houses; going on holidays; marrying and having children; should not be our all-consuming passions in life.

In verses 45 to 51 we see that our lifestyles should be conscientious. We should not take liberties by being irresponsible and pleasing ourselves; because we feel that there are not yet serious signs of the Lord's second coming. He will come suddenly and that should be our main expectation from day to day as we toil, rejoice, relax and potter through our lives. These things are all just temporary and not worthy of our entire focus.

III
Filled and rained upon

Around the same time as I had the above visions, I had a vision about rain. I saw rain falling and this rain looked like lemonade, with hail resembling ice cubes, laced through it.

In our spiritual lives we all at times go through periods of being dry. Nothing new happens. We do not know whether we are happy or not and we do not really sense God's presence. At least; not in the way we expect to.

At a difficult and unhappy time like this, the sudden awareness of the Lord's presence is just as refreshing as that outpouring of rain in the vision, or an ice-laced glass of lemonade on a dry, hot day!

It is not often that we recognize ourselves to be in "spiritual drought", as such. Only when we walk into a place of genuine worship, will we realize this, as we may break down and weep, because we notice that we have come in from the cold, hostile world out there. We may also break down when we realize that we do not really have joy in our lives. The powerful presence of the Holy Spirit will be a great relief and comfort then.

We can however, create an atmosphere of true worship whilst on our own out there. We can turn off the radio; television; people's voices; etcetera; so that we can just begin to sing to God. It may even be just a simple tune which we can sing over and over. Then, in the stillness and with the worship, we will sense the awesome and empowering presence of God. He will just come and embrace us.

These periods must become programmed into our awareness, for our daily routine. We do not need reminders in the form of chaos or despair.

Please study the spiritual significance in Psalm 65 verses 1 to 13. Verses 1 to 5 share about our blessings, which come from confessing our sins and being chosen by God to share in his privileges. Verses 6 to 8 portray the greatness of God, by viewing the wonders of his deeds in creation.

Verses 9 to 13 show the greatness of creation, due to a wondrous outpouring of rain in nature. It is dramatic and awesome.

In nature rain brings about the growth of many wonderful and beautiful plants. Sometimes we did not even know about the existence of some of them. Then all sorts of wonderful and colorful birds come to grace the scene and make it even more beautiful.

In a spiritual context the outpouring of, or anointing by the Holy Spirit makes us experience strengths, beauty and gifts we always knew of and others we did not even know about.

So we should allow for a generous outpouring of the Holy Spirit upon our lives regularly. The Holy Spirit is constantly inside of us as believers, but we also need to be bathed into his presence, or we will remain dull and lifeless and become burdened by our troubles, even though we read the word of God. The Holy Spirit should be active in us or we will not be able to understand or obey the Bible. This means that we should interact with the Holy Spirit and not ignore him. Pray and wait upon him to touch you and thereby anoint you.

A plant usually contains water on the inside yet, if it is not regularly watered it would die. So we need to be regularly bathed into the presence of the Holy Spirit or we will die spiritually. Our anointing will fade away.

The Holy Spirit is the evidence of God's presence. He is also God, so we should not refer to him as "it". We must acknowledge his presence in and around us and not go around with an attitude of ignoring him and taking him for granted. He is here for a purpose. He is the Comforter and the Helper whom Jesus sent for us.

We need to be bathed into his presence in the same way in which he descended upon Jesus, to baptize him spiritually, on the day when Jesus was baptized in water. Jesus is also God himself. That is why he did not bring the Holy Spirit to the world permanently, while he was still in it himself. He promised the Comforter when he left the world and the Holy Spirit descended upon his disciples on the Day of Pentecost, afterwards.

We as Christians cannot survive only on the outpouring we received on the day when we were saved or baptized. We also cannot survive on the outpouring which the disciples received. That was for them then. We need our own now and on a regular basis. If we have been experiencing a spiritual winter period in our lives, we cannot be revived by recalling an incident which occurred twenty years ago, when we were baptized in the Holy Spirit and were filled with love, peace and joy. We need a fresh baptism. Like a plant needs regular watering. We cannot live on memories.

In order to live productive lives as Christians, we need the Helper who is also the Comforter, because yes, we do need practical assistance, advice and guidance to solve our problems and understand our situations from day to day. Sometimes we need miracles as well.

When we are down-hearted; pressurized; depressed and lonely, we need the Holy Spirit and he does come when we ask him to enter a room, a building or ourselves. He touches us when we ask him to. He is inside of us, but we also need his empowering presence around us, to embrace us. We need him inside of us, in order to speak to us, bind the broken pieces of our hearts and heal us from inner disease. We need him around us, so that we may be empowered to do great things.

This is what Jesus came to do on earth, but now he does it all through the Holy Spirit. Jesus was in one place at a time. The Holy Spirit can be everywhere around the world at the same time and when he is there, we should acknowledge his presence and allow him to work and move amongst us. If we do not ask him to perform certain actions, he will not do them for us. He is not only there as a seal of our salvation; because then we can ignore him and take him for granted, as if he was a seal on an envelope.

When we are indecisive about something, require knowledge, need wisdom or are worried about something, we should ask his practical assistance. He is not simply in our minds like a form of thought or psychological reasoning. He can be there in the same way as Jesus was on earth—walking beside us as our friend. Otherwise we will simply become dry Christians who only respond to need and crisis.

We should be alive in the Holy Spirit, because we should communicate with him as we would with a trusted, reliable friend who listens, answers and helps. Read John 16 verses 4 to 15. If we ignore him he will not force himself on us, but if he knows that we are actively seeking him, he will be gracious and forthcoming. If we need him desperately, he will be there in a more powerful way. Most of all; we should never underestimate him, because he has the power to do the most amazing things. Greater things than we can ever imagine or expect. He is all-powerful!

CHAPTER THIRTY ONE

I
A happy family

Happiness is an asset which seems elusive at the times when we feel that we need it most. We are constantly aware of the things we lack and then we also automatically notice how other people seem to own the exact possession which we ourselves need. This state of mind can lead to bitterness and that is exactly the opposite attitude to what we need to possess, if we want to move forwards and establish
our own sense of contentment.

Sometimes, as we walk past people in the supermarkets, shopping malls and parks we wonder what their lives are like at home. At certain times we drive past folk on their way to the cinema or restaurants and we feel that they represent the image of perfection and we desire to be like them. We want the joy; peace and money which they appear to have. We feel left out.

Yet, is what we see a picture of reality, or is it an illusion? Consider the following:

Scene 1

Visions of Jesus

A small group of people is playing in a garden. The mother is carrying a little girl, of about two years old, in her arms. A little boy who is about five years old, is standing next to them. The three of them are playing with a kitten. In the same pretty garden a short distance away, is the father observing them with a smile, from near the gate.

This little family seems happy and they resemble the picture of perfection, from the outside.

The true facts of the situation are as follows: The children are not siblings, but cousins. The man is not the father of either one of the children. He is a family friend, who loves children and does not mind playing with them. The mother of the little girl is only partially happy at this moment. Her husband is not out there with her in the garden. He went off somewhere with his friends, to watch a game of sport. So then, deep inside, the woman is not happy with him. He does not spend much time with her. However, she does not confide this to her extended family, or to her gay friend, who is in the garden with her now.

The little boy's mother dropped him off there, because his father is the brother of the woman in the garden, but he has not been paying regular child maintenance. As a result—in a fit of desperation—his ex-girlfriend left the boy (their son) on his aunt's doorstep, as an act of punishment to the father. This picture then—as you would agree—does not represent a picture of perfect joy.

So what is this yearning we have to be part of someone else's family; or to be just like them; or have the same material possessions as them; or to possess the love which they seem to enjoy?

In most cases, what we see is only an illusion and the truth is far removed from that. Yet we will stake everything we have on what we've just seen, until we learn the actual facts.

Scene 2
A husband may be thrown into a jealous rage over something he thought he saw. A girlfriend can grab her belongings and hurriedly move to another city, merely because of following a false lead, which came from something she has seen or heard, with a few coincidental events thrown in to make it look real. In this manner people who do not have a firm relationship with God, can ruin their own lives, or jeopardize the lives of other people.

Scene 3
A woman may have a husband who usually works late and on the day when he finishes at work earlier, she may coincidentally see him at a shopping mall, chatting to the girlfriend of a colleague. This lady might be new in the neighborhood, seeking information. She might also be a ballet teacher on her way home from lessons (still dressed in a leotard and a pair of jeans). He has already met her previously, in an innocent manner and yet the only things his wife will focus on at this moment are: his friendly facial expression and the other lady's trim figure.

If the wife does not mention seeing him chatting to this woman, he might also not mention her, because he does not know that his wife has seen them together. His wife may then assume that he gets off from work early every day. This can lead to an attitude of suspicion and low self-esteem on the part of the wife. Such a situation can then cause real problems. Meanwhile, the reason for her attitude was never mentioned and there was never any actual problem with her husband.

Scene 4
A lonely young girl may see a man in a restaurant with a bouquet of flowers, which he wants to present to his female companion. This girl observing them has a feeling that this would never happen to her. Yet, the man might be making up for bad behavior or unfaithfulness. His wife on the other hand, might see the young girl sitting by herself at a table and feel threatened by the thought that this girl might become her husband's new love interest.

If we start seeing ourselves as fortunate though, we will realize that we possess certain gifts which someone else would pay a fortune for. This realization would immediately put us at ease. We would be smiling and singing with gratitude. We all possess something which not everybody else has. We should recognize this attribute as a blessing and thank God for it, daily.

II
Your calling

I received the following interpretation to a tongue, while I was ministering to a young believer once. He was on the brink of a beautiful ministry, at the beginning of 1999. The interpretation was as follows:

"Son, go and make disciples of all men as I shall lead you and I will be your God, your father and your mother. I will provide for you in everything that you may ever desire or think of. Be to me the son that you were born to be. I will bless your children and their children. Just walk in my light;

in my paths of righteousness and I will always be a beacon of light to your steps and to your way, to direct your footsteps.

Stand aside, so that I will take over and give to you and to your family all the blessings I have in store for you; blessings without end, from morning till night. I will shine before you and go before you.

Come child follow me, because you are mine and I love you. I made you in my image and I bought you. You are what I desire and I should be what you desire and then I will give you more, much more than you can ask or think of, both now and even unto everlasting.

My grace will always be sufficient for you and you will abound in grace towards others, as long as you follow in my footsteps. I go before you and at times I will walk beside you.

With me all things are possible and you need not fear to ask anything of me. Just continue to bless and to honor my Name and my Word will be fulfilled in you, my child."

It was a tremendous blessing for me to be of service with regards to the delivering of this message.

III
Definition of the number Twelve

For some divine purpose, the number twelve comes up several times in the Bible. Just as does the number seven.

In Luke 9 verses 12 to 17 we have the episode of the five loaves and the two fishes which Jesus multiplied manifold times. There were leftovers enough to fill twelve baskets.

This number sounds natural, because each one of the twelve disciples who were with Jesus, must have been carrying a basket with them already for their own use. The supernatural aspect of this, is that these baskets were supposed to be empty at this time and yet they each contained leftovers. This is the overflow of the blessings of food.

There was also Jairus' daughter, who was very ill and died. Jesus raised her from the dead. Read Luke 8 verses 41 to 56. She was about twelve years old when she experienced what might have been the greatest event of her life.

When Jairus met up with Jesus, it was at the time when Jesus was also reached by the woman who had been suffering from an issue of blood for twelve years. This means that her suffering began at around the same time as when Jairus' daughter was born.

Another instance is when, according to Jewish custom, a boy or girl is a child up to the age of twelve. Thereafter, from the age of thirteen onwards they are regarded as men and women. The age of twelve is then the sign that childhood is ending.

Jacob had twelve sons and they later formed the twelve tribes of Israel, (God had changed Jacob's name to Israel).

In Exodus 28 verse 9 we have the names of the twelve sons of Israel, which are to be engraved on the two onyx stones. Read verses 15 to 21. In verse 21 we see that there also have to be twelve other stones. One for each tribe of Israel.

A significant point about the twelve tribes of Israel, is the fact that the number of Jews who will be saved by Grace from eternal damnation in hell, is twelve times the tribes of Israel multiplied by one thousand: 144 thousand Jews. Revelation 7 verses 4 to 8.

Revelation 4 verse 10 speaks about the 24 elders, which is two times the number twelve. The precious stones are mentioned again in Revelation 21 verse 19 and they are twelve in number. Verse 21 speaks about the twelve gates, which are pearls.

Revelation 21 verse 16 speaks about the heavenly city, which is 120 000 (twelve times ten thousand) furlongs in length; in width and in height. The wall in verse 17 is 144 cubits thick. This is twelve times twelve cubits.

All this shows the divine significance of the number twelve and one day its significance might be revealed even more completely. It is a number which defines completion and predestined order.

*

A note of encouragement for those who are facing serious trials: You shall not be ashamed. Read Matthew 5 verse 11; Isaiah 41 verse 11; Isaiah 42 verses 1 and 2 and Exodus 23 verses 20 to 28.

CHAPTER THIRTY TWO

I
The way up

On the 14th of January 1999 I had a vision of Jesus, on a high mountain. A group of believers and myself were on our way up the mountain. The blooms of the plants growing there, were covered with snow. Angels which were the color of gold, came down the mountain, while we were halfway up and handed us each a grain of corn. I studied the corn and inside it there was a baby. It was the same with the other grains of corn. The babies each had a Bible in their hands. I saw that these Bibles were coming from the hearts of the babies.

In this vision Jesus is at the top of the mountain and we are on our way up. Clearly this illustrates that Jesus is at the top of spirituality. He is perfect. We are still on our way there, as we try to overcome sin, doubt, fear and sickness. The mountain is high in altitude, that is why the blooms are covered with snow.

Jesus has our best interests at heart, so he sends ministering angels to aid us in our quest towards perfection. These angels might not be visible to us, but they are out there, where we least expect them. I feel that we should be aware of their existence, because they are there at God's command.

Corn signifies a harvest. In Biblical terms we can speak about a harvest of souls. Inside the corn from the vision, we find an infant. Read John 4 verses 31 to 41.

This shows me that while we harvest souls for God's kingdom, we will beget spiritual babies, who are even further from perfection than we are, because they are still starting out on their journey, up the mountain. God places these newly born-again souls into our hands, so that we can be responsible for them. These babies already have a part of God's word in them (the Bibles), because they heard it before they repented from sin.

This word is in their hearts when they receive Jesus. Then they need to take it into their hands, in order to study it and make it their own. Thereafter they can tell others about their newfound salvation. Read Psalm 119 verses 1 to 16.

At this point however, they are still very new and vulnerable in their faith, so they need our care and concern, or we will be held accountable if they get lost. So, while we go through trials we should still remember to take care of the new believers. Read Luke 15 verses 1 to 10.

They still value the Word very much, that is why it is hidden in their hearts—according to the vision I had.

II
Royal gown colors and fabric

I often have visions about the garments Jesus wears. I had one of him wearing a gown of emerald and sapphire blue colors. These colors on the gown resemble those jewels in their brilliance. This means that the material of his gown is like silk or satin. There are also various yellow prints on the gown. Each print is about 3 cm by 6 cm in size. This vision portrays Jesus in a royal setting. He is dressed like a king.

III
Frozen growth

In another vision I saw Jesus standing before a frozen fountain. He seems to be willing it to thaw, by the power of his love.

From this vision we see that even when we are spiritually indifferent, God is still there, because the frozen fountain represents us as cold Christians. God is still a reality here. Therefore he can melt the ice and make us feel love again. You may be cold, but you are not abandoned. So you should also not abandon those who need your love. Ask the Lord to warm you up, because He is faithful. He can deal with your pain.

CHAPTER THIRTY THREE

I
Strange planets

Our universe remains interesting. So much must still be uncovered about the development of our various galaxies. The universe out there is unfathomably vast and yet God still finds human beings of enough interest for him to spend his time on us. He still wants us to become one with him and he still wants us to accept his love.

In the year 2011 I began to have a series of very awe-inspiring dreams about God placing me on other, unknown, but inhabitable planets. At least; I could live in the body I occupied when I was there.

The big challenge in these dreams was the fact that I was alone on these planets (no other human beings were there) and I would see several moons and other planets close by (with the naked eye).

So all this would make me feel completely overwhelmed and I would be filled with a sense of unworthiness at being so close to God (because it would be only myself and Him out there).

So each time in the dream I would tell God that this was too much for me, a mere mortal. He did not pay attention to my words or say anything to me, though. I did not look at him directly, but I could sense his very powerful presence. So then I often fell on my knees and begged for this to end.

Sometimes I would be alone on one planet and I would see my younger sister on another planet, also sitting alone. The numerous moons surrounding the foreign planet I occupied, really used to frighten me.

In the year 2012 I had a dream in which I was with a friend and we saw a half moon in the sky. Close to it was the bottom half of a totally red planet and this planet was something new in our skies. It was also visible to the naked eye. My friend told me not to be alarmed and to just stop looking at this scene in the sky.

I feel that this new planet signifies a new season for the world as we know it. Our outlook on life should change drastically. We should be ready for change.

I believe these dreams about the planets were intended for me to know that God sees us each as if we were the only person on earth. He has all the time in the world for us, therefore he expects us to be completely intimate with him. So spend time alone with God's Word. He will speak to you like never before.

Also, there will be times when we are completely alone, with God as our only companion. This situation should not cause us to fear though (when we see other people being as distant as another planet). Here we are simply being set aside, for a divine purpose, which we might not yet be aware of. This would not happen if it was not for our future benefit.

II
Signs in the sky

Prior to the above-mentioned dream (about the red planet), I have had many dreams about other strange objects appearing in our skies, as well as about words written in the sky, during the year 2012. I did not understand those words, because they were foreign. In these dreams I would be so filled with the fear of God, whilst hoping that nothing drastic would ensue.

During these dreams I was completely convinced about the rapture. By the middle of the year 2012, I had seen more than twenty of these colorful signs and objects in our sky during my dreams. I do not understand why God chose to give me these dreams, but I am humbled by the experience.

So we should walk circumspectly and be aware of the fact that God is holy and indeed very great. He can do anything. We should also realize that the end of days could be very near.

So do try to make time for God during your busy day. It is the most important item to have on your schedule.

CHAPTER THIRTY FOUR

I
A personal touch from God

Sometimes God's grace comes unexpectedly, at a moment when we need it most; when we may find that we are too weak to help ourselves any further. We might also be too weak to pray.

I was once laying down on my bed, very weak after suffering from severe pains and bleeding for hours on end. Suddenly, a hand started to tickle my abdomen. I began to laugh, but I was half asleep and did not open my eyes. So I said: "stop it" but the tickling continued. Then I saw a hand move around above my head and because I was not fully awake I tried to bite at it, but it avoided my mouth. After a while I woke up fully and realized that God had chosen to reach down and touch me with his healing hand. This was to signify that I was going to be healed completely. I rested peacefully afterwards and woke up refreshed.

On another occasion I was awoken from my sleep by being lifted off my bed and into the air. Then a voice spoke into my ear for a long time, in words which I could not understand. I was horizontally held there in the air, for a considerably long time, with something like winds surrounding me and then finally lowered back onto my bed.

Then the being I recognized to be God, held me very tightly and for so long a period, that I told Him I was a mere human being and would thus die from such an intense experience.

The following day I could still feel the waves of His love going through me, physically.

After such experiences one feels so completely aware of God's love and ultimate concern. So we should never doubt him when times are tough. He really wants us to know that he cares for us deeply and this is why we should realize that he will always come through for us.

So, if you have any doubts about God's concern for your life, do feel free to pray about this and ask him to strengthen your faith. Be firm in this.

II
Healing through an angel

I was once going through a day of deep emotional disappointment and hurt. I have had to let go of something very precious.

On the night of this experience I was awoken from my sleep by an angel who was so huge and tall, that her height reached past the ceiling level of the bedroom, but I saw her entire form. She was dressed in a purple robe and she had long, curly, auburn hair. She looked deliriously happy and so she just began to laugh, while looking at me. She had stars in her eyes. It seemed as if she wanted to teach me to laugh at my pain. Her laughter had a musical sound; like bells ringing. She laughed with tremendous joy, for a very long period. Then she began to praise the Lord. I watched her for a while and then joined her in praising the Lord. She continued with praises for what felt like hours, until I fell asleep from exhaustion.

When I awoke the following morning I was completely healed of my emotional distress. I had never experienced such instant emotional healing before.

It is not often that God will command an angel to come and comfort us in this way. So the mere memory of this experience should serve as healing in itself. We should praise God through our deepest pain and this will bring eventual healing. May God bless you and keep you strong.

III
Spiritual growth

It is important to maintain one's spiritual growth in the same manner as we maintain our bodies. We feed our souls through the reading of God's Word. We exercise spiritually; when we pray and intercede for ourselves and others.

1. We grow by doing more, in whatever our ministry of choice happens to be.

2. We grow by being more mature in our reactions to certain challenges in our lives. Things like personal attacks, for example.

3. We grow through experience, so our responses to setbacks and trials becomes more mature. We are not as easily derailed as before.

4. We also grow when we lay at the Lord's feet and soak in his presence during worship. In this way we learn to know his heart for people and situations in life. We learn to hear his voice and his instruction. We can discern his voice from any other voice. We learn to identify foreign spirits and we learn to discern the truth from a lie. We also gain our healing in this way.

5. As we grow we also learn to work with others in ministry and to die to self. We allow our character to be shaped by others, as well as by the word of God. We learn to love more and to be more tolerant where we need to be. But as we grow, we also learn to be less tolerant of sin and everything which is an abomination to God. We do not tolerate sin in our own lives and we correct those who do wrong, but with love.

6. We also grow by praying more in the spirit (when we pray in tongues). Sometimes our usual language is not sufficient to deal with evil spirits, which we may sometimes sense around us. If we lack the words to pray, we should pray in tongues, until we can discern the nature of the actual situation which we may be confronted with. If no revelation comes, we should continue to pray in tongues, until we sense that the oppression has lifted. If you are born-again, but cannot pray in tongues, you should ask your spiritual leaders to lay hands on you and pray for you to receive the gift.

IV
Words of encouragement

I trust that your journey through this book has brought you closer to God. If so, then please share your experiences with others and encourage them as well. Keep revising the book, so that you will remain spiritually on track.

Remember to read the scriptures mentioned and continually study the Bible, so that God can speak to you as well.

Always be aware of the fact that your personal testimony counts and that it can change another life. So never hide your testimony. It is your Christian duty to share it.

Do not hide your gifts and talents. Work hard at them, pray over them and do not give up. You will succeed in the end. Trust God throughout your challenges and your light will remain shining. People remember those who held on against the odds, not those who gave up. Dedicate everything you undertake to the Lord and trust him. Also trust his timing. Read Proverbs 3 verses 5 and 6.

We all have a purpose in life and it is important to know how important it is. Our purpose in life is useful to us as well as to some other people in the world. So we should not allow any individual or force to keep us from fulfilling our life's purpose.

If you know that there is something unique in your future, it is important to cultivate your gifts and talents, faithfully. Also, if you have received a prophesy which says that you are going to attain something exceptional in the future, it is important to keep this word to yourself, unless it was delivered in public.

Try not to cause anybody to become jealous of you, because then they will certainly attempt to derail you and keep you from achieving your God-ordained destiny.

If you have any special goals for the future, discuss them with the Lord only. People are not always strong enough to rejoice in your blessings, or in your plans to do well in the future.

While you work on improving yourself in life; by working hard on your gifts and talents, it is important to remember that these should glorify God at all times. They should serve his purposes and show that you worship him. Remain humble no matter how successful you are in life. When the going gets tough; remember that nothing good comes easily. If you persist to the outmost, you will receive a great and lasting reward. Nobody will be able to take it away and those who mocked you, will be ashamed. Read Zephaniah 3 verse 19 and 20.

Ask the Lord to reveal your purpose to you. Mainly it will stem from the cultivating of a special talent you have. Some talents are recognized very early in life, while others show up as we mature. You will just find that you receive recognition for excelling way above others in a certain discipline. It may even come from your performance in your place of work.

Psalms 118 verse 25: Lord, save us! Lord, grant us success!

AUTHOR BIOGRAPHY

Brief autobiography

Personal testimony

I am a 52 year old South African lady. I grew up attending the Evangelical Bible Church in Swaziland. My growing up years were spent in Swaziland and I lived there until the age of eleven. I continued attending the EBC church after I moved with my parents to Pretoria, South Africa, where there was a branch of the church. Later, at the age of thirty, I joined a charismatic (pentecostal) church. This is where I got baptized in the Holy Spirit, began to speak in tongues and began to have my first visions.

The first vision I had was of Jesus; much larger than life, towering above the congregation of 3000 plus church attendants and it must have lasted a full hour. In the vision all He did was laugh. It was a laughter of triumph, peace, joy, as well as love. The love and laughter were in His eyes. It was as if He was telling me: "forget all these troubles around you. Just laugh at them!"

For the entire duration of this vision, tears were streaming down my face. I realized that when I turned around, I could still see Him in front of me, yet at the same time I also saw Him in front of me, when I returned to my previous position of standing; facing the stage. All the while He was still towering up in the air, above the congregation.

After this experience I discovered (the following morning at home), that an egg-sized uterine tumor which I previously had, was gone completely. It had stood out visibly for months, so it was easy to see that it was gone. In its place was a hollow which eventually evened out.

This was the beginning of my visions and inspired dreams. I would see what Jesus was doing inside the church. I would see what he was doing in a specific area of the church and I would observe the scenes he was revealing to me, for example: how he was healing somebody, or how he was comforting yet another person. I would also see Him during church cell (small group) meetings, where He would show me what His message was for the people who were present there. Many people received answers to their prayers and had their needs met in miraculous ways, at these cell meetings.

Miracle healing

One night, in January of the year 2002, I had a rupturing brain aneurysm and that night, within a matter of about five to ten minutes, I experienced the most excruciating pain I had ever known. It occurred in three different places. First in my forehead, as I bent to clean the bath tub—the blow felt like an axe striking me—then on the left side of my head, where the aneurysm was (it felt like my head was bursting there) and lastly in my left eye, which felt as if it was going to burst into a thousand pieces. There was just too much pain.

My mother, sister-in-law and fourteen year old nephew came to pray for me and without wasting time, my nephew rebuked the devil in Jesus' name. Immediately the entire rupturing process stopped. The intense pain was gone. I believe that I would have died if they had arrived a second too late. I myself was incapable of praying. All I could manage was: "God help me." Everything was happening so suddenly and frighteningly fast.

After this, the cut which had already started in the artery, began to bleed slowly (without my being aware of it). My body temperature shot up very high and my head became very hot. I began to vomit and this continued through the day and the night for the following couple of days.

I was very ill at my sister's home in Cape Town, after traveling by car whilst bleeding internally, all the way from Midrand (about a thousand kilometers away). I had travelled to Cape Town to attend my aunt's funeral with my mother, eldest brother and his wife. Thus I remained un-hospitalized for five days since I had become ill.

During this time I had developed blurred vision; double-sightedness and gradual paralysis. At the hospital which I went to eventually, the chief neurosurgeon arrived in the theatre just before the other, less experienced staff, attempted to take a chance at saving my life (the chances of that were very slim at the time). This surgeon left his other appointments to operate on me and he performed the surgery successfully. It was all a series of divine interventions. Without the surgery I would have died eventually, by the Wednesday of that week.

After surgery I learned to walk again. I had semi-vision in my right eye and total blindness in my left eye. This all improved, as the long weeks to my full recovery continued in very hot Cape Town weather. My full vision eventually returned after about six weeks.

At a certain stage during my convalescence I developed an allergic reaction to an antibiotic, which left me with burning skin for two weeks. The result of this was pock marks all over my body. This was the most horrendous experience of all, almost eclipsing everything else preceding it, but this also passed.

Writing background

I started writing fiction at the age of sixteen, but five years later, my manuscript of twelve chapters went missing.

About two months after my brain surgery, I began to read many large print books from the local library, because I could not read normal print at the time. Then I started paying attention to my Christian written material, which I had worked on during the previous year and which I believe should be read by everyone who will find the time to do so. I write about my spiritual dreams and visions. I give their interpretations for guidance and I add Biblical references to explain their significance according to the Word.

I also write and study Mathematics. I began my studies at the University of South Africa, with Mathematics and Physics as my majors, but did not complete them there. I continued studying on my own.

One month Journal

Day 1

YOU ARE SPECIAL…
because your DNA is similar to that of nobody else.

Your thoughts…

Day 2

YOU ARE SPECIAL...
because your hair is made especially for you. It is a gift, no matter how it looks.

Your thoughts...

Day 3

YOU ARE SPECIAL…

because your eyes are unique and God's eyes are upon you, constantly. Psalm 121 verse 5 and Ephesians 1 verses 17 and 18.

Your thoughts…

Day 4

YOU ARE SPECIAL…
because God knew you while you were still in your mother's womb. You are fearfully and wonderfully made. Psalms 139 verses 13 and 14.

Your thoughts…

Day 5

YOU ARE SPECIAL…

because your voice is unique to you and you can use it to praise God and to summon the presence of the Holy Spirit. When you call upon the Lord He will answer you. Jeremiah 33 verse 3.

Your thoughts…

Day 6

YOU ARE SPECIAL…
because you can choose to listen to the Word of God and to hear the voice of God. Mark 4 verse 23.

Your thoughts…

Day 7

YOU ARE SPECIAL...

because you may ask the Lord for wisdom. Proverbs 3 verse 13.

Your thoughts...

Day 8

YOU ARE SPECIAL…
because your skin color is not a mistake. It is a blessing.

Your thoughts…

Day 9

YOU ARE SPECIAL…

because everyday of the week you have a new chance to improve on the past.

Your thoughts...

Day 10

YOU ARE SPECIAL…
because everyday you have a new chance to forgive somebody.

Your thoughts…

Day 11

YOU ARE SPECIAL…
because everyday you have a new chance to love somebody.

Your thoughts...

Day 12

YOU ARE SPECIAL…
because everyday you can find someone to bless.

Your thoughts…

Day 13

YOU ARE SPECIAL...

because your perseverance in doing good can only make you happy. Proverbs 4 verse 18.

Your thoughts...

Visions of Jesus

Day 14

YOU ARE SPECIAL…
because you may ask the Lord for success. Proverbs 1 verse 7.

Your thoughts…

Day 15

YOU ARE SPECIAL…

because your heart and lungs work together to keep you alive.

Your thoughts…

Day 16

YOU ARE SPECIAL…
because while you are asleep, the Lord entertains you with dreams.

Your thoughts…

Day 17

YOU ARE SPECIAL…
because you have the right to choose the correct friends for your life. Proverbs 12 verse 26.

Your thoughts…

Day 18

YOU ARE SPECIAL…
because when you do right you are saved from trouble.
Proverbs 11 verse 8.

Your thoughts…

Day 19

YOU ARE SPECIAL…
because when you give freely you will have no regrets. Proverbs 11 verse 24.

Your thoughts…

Visions of Jesus

Day 20

YOU ARE SPECIAL…
because you can smile upon everyone, as a sign of a blessing to them and to improve their day. Proverbs 15 verse 13.

Your thoughts…

Day 21

YOU ARE SPECIAL…
because you can choose to be humble, everyday. Proverbs 18 verse 12.

Your thoughts…

Day 22

YOU ARE SPECIAL…

because you get a new chance to choose your words wisely everyday, so that you can speak life and not death. Proverbs 18 verse 21.

Your thoughts…

Day 23

YOU ARE SPECIAL…

because you get a chance to speak the truth, everyday.
Proverbs 9 verse 10.

Your thoughts…

Visions of Jesus

Day 24

YOU ARE SPECIAL…
because you can choose to keep your name clean. Proverbs 22 verse 1.

Your thoughts…

Day 25

YOU ARE SPECIAL…

because the Lord will not let you go hungry. Proverbs 10 verse 22.

Your thoughts…

Day 26

YOU ARE SPECIAL…
because you will thrive when you are corrected. Proverbs 10 verse 17.

Your thoughts…

Day 27

YOU ARE SPECIAL…

because when you are generous you will be rewarded with prosperity. Proverbs 11 verse 25.

Your thoughts…

Day 28

YOU ARE SPECIAL…
because you can choose to excel, regardless of whatever capacity you find yourself in.

Your thoughts...

Day 29

YOU ARE SPECIAL…

because when you are righteous, your home will be blessed. Proverbs 3 verse 33.

Your thoughts...

Day 30

YOU ARE SPECIAL…

because you can choose to be the bearer of good news. Proverbs 13 verse 17.

Your thoughts…

Day 31

YOU ARE SPECIAL…

because you can accept discipline every time, so that you will prosper through it. Proverbs 13 verse 18.

Your thoughts…

Visions of Jesus

Charlotte Patricia Lambert

Visions of Jesus

www.ingramcontent.com/pod-product-compliance
Lightning Source LLC
Chambersburg PA
CBHW071454040426
42444CB00008B/1335